WHO LIES THERE?

A Play in Three Acts

by

PHILIP JOHNSON

SAMUEL FRENCH LIMITED
LONDON

FOR AMATEUR PRODUCTION ENQUIRIES

UNITED KINGDOM AND WORLD EXCLUDING NORTH AMERICA
plays@SamuelFrench-London.co.uk
020 7255 4302/01

Each title is subject to availability from Samuel French, depending upon country of performance.

PERSONS OF THE PLAY

MRS FEARN

MRS BUTTERWORTH

FRANCIE

GEORGE

THE PROFESSOR

MADAM

MR MEAKIN

ALEC

MRS DUBINSKI

The Play happens in the back sitting-room of a house in Kensington, towards the end of the last century, on the late afternoon of a day in November, and the morning and afternoon of the following day.

WHO LIES THERE?

ACT I

SCENE.—*The back sitting-room in Kensington. Only just in Kensington, though: a stone's throw distance, and one would be in Earl's Court. The time is the late afternoon of a day in November, towards the end of the last century. The house is one of a small row, and the road in which it is situated is known as the Medway Passage: one of the very minor arteries of London, and only open to vehicular traffic at one end, where it joins the Earl's Court Road. At the other end it narrows to a passage between tall houses, along which pedestrians may proceed into the Cromwell Road.*

The room is of fair size, with the fireplace in the middle of the R. *wall, and the one door upstage* C. *When this door is open, one sees the narrow hallway which leads to the rest of the house, and, immediately opposite, another door which admits to the cellar. When this is open, one sees nothing but the black darkness of the cellar-head, the steps which descend to the cellar itself being just offstage* R., *and of course invisible to the audience. In the middle of the* L. *wall is a large french window. Through this one has a glimpse of the garden—backyard would describe it better—and a few sooty branches of a plane tree.*

The furniture is of the heavy style of the period. Slightly to L. *of* C. *is a round table, over which is draped a cloth of dark red chenille with a ball-fringed edge. To* L., *above, and* R. *of this are stiff-backed, horsehair-seated chairs. Slightly upstage of the fireplace is an easy chair, with, in front of it, a beaded footstool. Just below the fireplace, almost against the wall, at an angle to face towards up stage* L., *is an armchair. Against the back wall,* L. *of the door, is a sideboard, and upon this are several vases, a tantalus, a silver-plated cake-dish, an egg-cup-stand, a reading lamp, and various other silver-plated pieces which one instinctively feels are wedding presents. To* R. *of the door, against the wall, is a glass-fronted bookcase, and on top of it a marble bust of some unknown personage which has probably been "picked up at a sale". Against the wall, below the french window, is a horsehair-upholstered sofa, with very new-looking cushions. On the mantelshelf is a glass-encased clock, flanked on either side by prancing equestrian figures in bronze, and two or three smaller vases, while over the mantelshelf is a dark and somewhat sombre-looking landscape in oils, with a heavy gilt frame. In the upstage* R. *corner of the room is a standard-lamp with a fringed shade. At the french window are curtains and pelmet of some dark red material. Other chairs should be set about at the discretion of the producer. The room in general has an unlived-in air about it: there are no books or newspapers lying about, no work-baskets, no dents in the cushions: everything in it seems set and fixed . . . waiting.*

When the Curtain *rises* Mrs Fearn *is on her knees in front of the fireplace. She is about sixty, thin and quite unremarkable-looking. Upon her head is a sort of half-hat, half-bonnet, and her jacket is flung over the back of the easy chair. She rises immediately and goes into the passage and off* l.*, then returns directly with a pair of bellows. She kneels again by the fire and blows at it. In front of the table, considerably down stage, is a cylindrical-shaped object wrapped in brown paper. The french window stands open, and through it comes the sound of a contralto voice singing scales. The door, too, is open and, facing it across the passage, the cellar door is plainly seen. This, at first, is closed, and remains so for a moment or two. Then, slowly, without making the slightest sound, it opens, revealing the pitch blackness of the cellar-head.* Mrs Fearn *pauses for a moment, gives the fire a final puff, then rises to her feet and hangs the bellows on a hook by the side of the fireplace. This done, she turns and starts to look round the room. The sound of the scales suddenly impinges upon her, and, crossing quickly to the french window, she closes it, shutting out the sound. Then, remembering the paper-wrapped object, she bustles down to it and, stripping the paper from it, exposes a china, drainpipe-shaped umbrella-stand, a fearsome-looking thing, painted with a design of storks and water-lilies. Stepping back, she permits herself to be lost in admiration for a moment; then, bustlingly again, she whisks up the paper from the floor, and, folding it, goes to the sofa, lifts the cushions, and tucks the paper behind it. As she does so, a knock is heard at the front door. She hesitates a second, then starts on her way to answer it. In the passage she hesitates again, this time before the phenomenon of the open cellar door. Just for a moment she is puzzled, startled even. The knock is repeated. Hastily, she closes the cellar door, and goes off* r. *There is a very short pause, and then the sound of voices* Mrs Fearn's *and that of another woman.*

Mrs Fearn (*off*). Do come inside for a moment, won't you? This way. I've just been seeing to the fire.

(*She reappears and comes down* r.c.*, followed by* Mrs Butterworth. *The latter is also about sixty: a short, dumpling-shaped woman, with scraped-back hair, steel-rimmed spectacles, wearing a white apron with shoulder-straps over her blouse and skirt. She is carrying a plate upon which is a pile of oat-cakes. Her accent when she speaks is North of England. She comes to* r. *of* Mrs Fearn.)

Mrs Butterworth. I hope as you'll excuse me. I've no wish to intrude, I'm sure, but, as I says to Alec, "I do believe as them new folk next door has just arrived, and mebbe they'll have nothing in for their teas. I've a good mind", I says, "to nip round with a two-three of my oat-cakes, and chance it."

Mrs Fearn. Why—why, really, I'm sure that's very kind of you, Mrs—er——

Mrs Butterworth. Butterworth. Mrs Joe Butterworth, though the Joe part of it's been dead fourteen years come Burnley Wakes. Fatty heart.

Mrs Fearn. Burnley—let me see, that's up in the North, isn't it?

Mrs Butterworth. Aye. Lancashire. I come from there well-nigh thirty year ago, when I were married. Folk used to say they could tell I come from North by the way I spoke, but of course I've lost all that. I'm a proper Londoner now, I reckon. Oh, aye, a proper Cockney.

Mrs Fearn. Yes, of course. . . . But it *is* good of you. Shall I . . . ?

Mrs Butterworth (*giving her the plate of oat-cakes*). It's naught. Just 'appened to be my baking-day, that's all.

Mrs Fearn (*taking the plate*). Thank you so much. I'll just put them over here. Do sit down for a minute—won't you? They *do* look good, don't they? (*She takes them to the sideboard.*)

Mrs Butterworth (*sitting in the armchair*). Eaten real 'ot, and swimming in butter, with a dollop of golden syrup, and you'll none clem. . . . So we're to be neighbours, seemingly.

Mrs Fearn (*placing the plate on the sideboard*). Well—well, not exactly. It's my daughter and son-in-law who are coming to live here. They got married a week ago, and they return from their honeymoon today—in fact, I'm expecting them any minute now.

Mrs Butterworth. There, now! A couple o' newly-weds in the Terrace! Eeh, well, that will be nice! The last we had was at Number eight—and they only said they was married—I'd my doubts—and, anyway, after a month they flitted.

Mrs Fearn (*coming down R. of the table*). Oh dear. But—surely —this is quite a respectable neighbourhood, isn't it?

Mrs Butterworth. Oh, aye, neighbourhood's right enough. You'll find a two-three wrong uns, choose where you go. But you've no cause to worry; your daughter'll have me next door one side (*indicating to her L.*) and Professor and Madam Parker on the other. (*She indicates to her R.*)

Mrs Fearn. Madam?

Mrs Butterworth. Her being a singer, you see. All concert singers are madams.

Mrs Fearn (*sitting R. of the table*). Oh—then it would be her I heard just now.

Mrs Butterworth. Aye. Not a bad voice, mind you, but getting past it. The husband, the professor, did school-teaching at one time. They're all right. She's all for dress, and their front-doorstep could be inches in muck before she'd be seen cleaning it —but they don't do no harm, and she's very kind-hearted.

Mrs Fearn. There are . . . just the two of them?

MRS BUTTERWORTH. Since they lost their lodger—or *paying guest* as they called her. A Miss Barrett. Eighty if she was a day, plenty o' brass, but all eccentrical. Used to go flapping about in a lot of old clothes you'd have been shamed to put on a scarecrow. And then, about eighteen months ago, she goes off to stay with a niece at Tunbridge Wells, and barely gets there before she's took ill and dies—leaving the professor and madam *quite* a little nest-egg, if you please.

MRS FEARN. There, now!

MRS BUTTERWORTH. Enough for 'em to buy their house, anyway. Some folks has all the luck. The only lodger I ever had cleared off with my watch and a garnet brooch; and when I opened his wardrobe door to see if he'd left aught behind, a hundred and thirty-seven empty bottles fell out on me.

MRS FEARN (*clicking her tongue sympathetically*). Tck! Tck! Tck! —Of course, they're quite *good* houses, these, I suppose?

MRS BUTTERWORTH. I've naught to complain of in mine. Well built. Good thick walls, you know. You could smash the place to bits, and not a sound be heard next door. Right good cellars, too.

MRS FEARN. The cellar. Yes . . . (*She looks towards the cellar door.*) It's shut now.

MRS BUTTERWORTH. Eh?

MRS FEARN. I'm sorry. I'm afraid I was thinking aloud. But it's the cellar door, you know. Every now and then, it opens— on its own—when there's no one near it, I mean. It's done it two or three times, and always when I haven't been looking at it. It's made me feel quite—you know—creepy, in a way. (*She gives a little laugh.*)

MRS BUTTERWORTH. Eh? (*With a short laugh.*) Go on with you! It's the catch isn't working, that's all. (*She rises and goes briskly out to the cellar door.*) Let's have a look! (*She opens the cellar door, then slams it to.*) There, that's it! (*As she returns into the room.*) Why, you'll be getting it into your head next there's summat wrong with the house! 'Aunted or some such hokey-pokey! (*She stands R.C.*)

MRS FEARN (*quickly*). Oh, no, not really. I'm a very matter-of-fact sort of person, I'm afraid.—Hush! Do I hear a cab stopping?

MRS BUTTERWORTH (*listening*). I don't hear aught.

MRS FEARN. I thought perhaps it was Francie and George. It's time they were here.

MRS BUTTERWORTH. Aye, and about time I made tracks for home, too, what's more.

MRS FEARN (*rising; hastily*). No, no, don't go. Stay and meet them. After all, you're going to be neighbours, you know . . .

MRS BUTTERWORTH. Oh, well, just a two-three minutes, then. (*As she catches sight of the umbrella-stand.*) Oh!—but isn't that *beautiful*! (*She comes down C. to the stand.*) Now, that's what *I* call "choice"!

Mrs Fearn (*pleased*). It is lovely, isn't it? A wedding present from Francie's Auntie Edith! Painted by herself! (*She moves down* R.)

Mrs Butterworth. Never! (*Examining it closer.*) Why, I bet the Queen herself'd snap at it for the lobby at Windsor, eh? Just look at them storks! That real, you almost expect 'em to quack!

Mrs Fearn. Francie's had some really wonderful presents. Even this very house itself!

Mrs Butterworth. No!

(*Slowly, and without any sound, the cellar door opens again.*)

Mrs Fearn. A present from George's uncle. And quite a lot of the furniture, too, what's more!

Mrs Butterworth (*crossing down* R. *to* Mrs Fearn). Eeh, well, that's something like a present, eh? (*She looks round the room.*) Real handsome furniture, too! Not the sort they give away with a pound o' tea—oh, no! (*She sees the open cellar door and pauses.*) Well, I'm——

Mrs Fearn. What——?

(*She follows the direction of* Mrs Butterworth's *look. There is a tiny pause. Then,* Mrs Butterworth, *jerking into action, marches up stage, and out into the passage. She steps into the darkness of the cellarhead and peers down into the cellar—that is, she looks downwards in the direction off* R.)

Mrs Butterworth (*calling*). Hey, you down there, whoever you are, let's have no more of your monkey tricks, d'you hear?

Mrs Fearn (*involuntarily*). Oh, don't! (*She moves a few steps up stage.*)

Mrs Butterworth (*emerging into the passage—with a broad grin*). Eeh, it was only my little joke! There's naught there! What could there be?

Mrs Fearn. Yes, I know, but . . .

Mrs Butterworth (*laughing*). I'd have looked a bit soft, though, if summat had answered me back, eh? (*She closes the door with a slam.*) I'll get my nephew, Alec, to come and have a look at this here catch. (*She comes back into the room to* c.) He's down with me from Burnley for a fortnight, and right clever with his hands.—Hush! There, now! *That's* a cab all right!

Mrs Fearn. Francie and George! (*She starts to hurry towards the doorway, then halts abruptly up* c.) No! No, I won't! They've got a key! They'll like to let themselves into their own house for the first time, won't they?

Mrs Butterworth (*her hands behind her back—struggling to untie her apron*). Eeh dear! And me in my apron! Drat the thing! (*She moves down* L.)

Francie (*off*). Mother! Mother, where are you?

(MRS BUTTERWORTH *whisks off her apron, and tosses it over the back of the chair* L. *of the table.*)

MRS FEARN (*calling*). I'm here, Francie, in here!

(FRANCIE *comes hurrying in. She is a pretty, rather frail-looking young woman in her very early twenties, wearing what is obviously her going-away costume, together with a fur-trimmed jacket and little fur-trimmed hat.*)

FRANCIE (*hurrying to* L. *of* MRS. FEARN—*throwing her arms about her—excitedly*). Mother! Did you think we were never coming? There was fog here and there, and the train was late! (*She kisses her.*) Darling, oh, how nice to see you! Oh, how nice!

MRS FEARN (*her hands on* FRANCIE'S *shoulders—holding her a little away from her*). Let me look at you!—Why, but you're not a bit sunburnt!

FRANCIE. In November? (*Hurrying on breathlessly.*) It rained nearly every day, and there was a wreck, and we saw the lifeboat put out, and an old lady was blown right over on the promenade —oh, and we heard Madam Patti at the Pavilion, and George and I had a *dreadful* quarrel on the second day, and I said I should come home to you, but of course I didn't mean to really!

MRS FEARN. Francie!

FRANCIE (*nodding quickly*). I cried over a book by Marie Corelli, and George said I was silly, and I must remember I was a married woman now, and act like one. I never thought he could have been so stern, but I rather liked it really—(*Seeing* MRS BUTTERWORTH *she breaks off.*) Oh——

MRS FEARN. This is Mrs Butterworth, dear, your next-door neighbour, and she's brought you some lovely oat-cakes!

FRANCIE (*shyly now; to* MRS BUTTERWORTH). Oh . . . but how very nice of you. (*She hesitates, then crosses down stage to her; holding out her hand.*) How-do-you-do?

MRS BUTTERWORTH (*grasping the hand and giving it a hearty shake*). Very pleased to meet you, luv. (*Still holding her hand.*) And listen to me: if there's aught I can do at any time, you're welcome, so don't be backward in coming forward, except twixt two and three of an afternoon, when I has my lie-down, see?

FRANCIE (*smiling*). Thank you.

(*There is a slight noise from the passage and* GEORGE *comes in. He is twenty-five, of quite pleasing though by no means striking appearance, and is wearing a great-coat and carrying his hat in his hand. He goes straight to* MRS FEARN *to her* L.)

GEORGE. Well, Mother, here we are, then! (*He kisses her.*) And how are you, eh?

MRS FEARN. Very well, George. But you look all hot, as though you'd been running.

GEORGE (*unwinding his scarf*). I've been having a row with the cabby, that's all. Thought he'd got a mug to deal with, I suppose, until I spoke a few quiet words and showed him different.

FRANCIE (*moving up to* L. *of* GEORGE; *admiringly*). Oh, George! (*She takes off her hat.*)

MRS BUTTERWORTH. Was it a hansom?

GEORGE. A growler.

FRANCIE. Oh—oh, this is Mrs Butterworth, George. She lives next door.

GEORGE (*coming down* C. *and crossing to* MRS BUTTERWORTH; *shaking hands*). How-do-you-do?

(FRANCIE *breaks* L.C. *above the table, puts her hat on the table, and starts to take off her jacket.*)

MRS BUTTERWORTH. Pleased to meet you. I only rode in a hansom once. All on my own I was, and it seemed to be me and the horse, and all the world against us. Never again!

FRANCIE. But—where are the bags, dear?

GEORGE (*taking off his great-coat*). In the passage. I'll carry them up later. (*He moves up* C.) Shall I take your things?

(*He slings his coat over one arm, takes* FRANCIE's *jacket and hat, and goes out up* C.)

FRANCIE (*catching sight of the umbrella-stand*). Oh! Oh, Mother! (*Hurrying down* L. *to it.*) Oh, but how *lovely*!

MRS FEARN. From Auntie Edith, dear.

FRANCIE (*rapturously—with clasped hands*). Oh *isn't* it beautiful! (*Calling.*) George! George, do come and look! (*She kneels beside it.*) Look! Look, she's actually painted a dear little butterfly!

(GEORGE *enters up* C.)

MRS FEARN (*crossing to the fire; to* MRS BUTTERWORTH). Auntie Edith was always the artistic one. A spinster, you know. (*She pokes the fire.*)

MRS BUTTERWORTH. I don't wonder. (*She crosses to* MRS FEARN.) What should she want with a man, when she can do things like that on her own?

GEORGE (*coming down* L.). Very nice. An umbrella-stand, eh?

FRANCIE (*rising from her knees*). It's *much* too beautiful to keep umbrellas in, isn't it?

(*At this point, the figure of a man appears at the french window: a tall man who, thrusting his face against the glass, peers into the room.*)

MRS BUTTERWORTH. If it were mine, I'd have bulrushes in it —half a dozen, thrust in careless-like!

FRANCIE (*crossing to* L. *of* MRS BUTTERWORTH; *eagerly*). Bulrushes! I must find out at once where I can get some, and put them on my shopping list!

GEORGE. Where will you have it? Out in the passage?

FRANCIE. No, no! Somewhere where we can see it!

MRS FEARN (*indicating the corner up* L.). What about up there, near the window? (*Turning, she sees the figure outside the window and gives a little scream.*) Oh!

(*The others, startled by her exclamation, look towards the window.*)

FRANCIE (*coming down* L. *of* GEORGE *and grasping his arm*). George! —George, who is it?

MRS BUTTERWORTH (*almost simultaneously*). It's all right! It's all right. It's only the Professor! (*Shouting and beckoning towards the figure.*) Come on in, Professor! Come in! (*To the others.*) Eeh dear, you'd think I owned the blessed place, eh?

(*During the last sentence, the* PROFESSOR *has opened the window. He is in the late fifties: a tall, thin, loose-jointed man, with long arms and legs, and hair and moustache that have been sandy, but are now turning to grey. Both in manner and speech, he is somewhat dry and over-precise. And now:*)

THE PROFESSOR (*one foot in the room—turning and speaking to someone off*). It's all right, Mildred! Mrs Butterworth's here! (*He comes into the room.*) Really but this is most unconventional. I do hope that you'll forgive us, but we——

MRS BUTTERWORTH. Nay, man, there's no call for ceremony! Come and meet your new neighbours! (*Indicating* MRS FEARN.) This is Mrs—what *is* your name, luv?

(THE PROFESSOR *moves above the table.* MADAM *appears outside the french window.*)

MRS FEARN (*a shade confusedly.*) Er—Mrs Fearn. (*She crosses to* THE PROFESSOR.)

MRS BUTTERWORTH (*going down* R.; *as* MADAM *steps into the room*). And here's Madam!

(MADAM *steps in and remains by the window.* MADAM *is a few years younger than the* PROFESSOR—*but only a very few. She, too, is tall, but built on rather more generous lines. Her walk is inclined to be stately, and her gestures are occasionally reminiscent of the concert platform. She is wearing a somewhat over-elaborate afternoon dress, with rather a lot of lace and bead trimming, and a long tulle scarf is draped over her head, then wound loosely round her throat, the ends floating down behind her. Her voice when she speaks is rich and vibrant.*)

THE PROFESSOR (*shaking hands with* MRS FEARN). How-do-you-do? Welcome! Welcome to our midst, dear lady!

MRS BUTTERWORTH. Come on in, Madam! Don't be shy! The more the merrier!

(MADAM *moves towards* C. *below the table.*)

Mrs Fearn (*a little overwhelmed by the* Professor's *manner*). Thank you, but—er—it's my daughter and son-in-law who are coming to live here.

The Professor. Ah! (*He turns to* Francie *and* George.) Welcome, indeed, to both of you! (*He indicates* Madam.) My wife!

Madam (*turning and advancing upon* Francie *and* George— *holding out her hand at arm's length*). Such a pleasure! How-do-you-do?

(George *and* Francie *shake hands with her,* George *a shade over-heartily,* Francie *very shyly, both murmur conventional greetings.*)

Mrs Butterworth. And in case you haven't guessed, just fresh from their honeymoon! (*To* Francie.) Now, now, there's no need to colour up.

Madam. Not really! But how very charming!

The Professor (*with rather pompous gallantry*). And the very thing the Terrace lacked! Youth and romance! A little touch of *Primavera,* eh?

Madam (*crossing in front of the* Professor *to* L. *of* Mrs Fearn; *advancing with her arm extended as before*). Do forgive me. How-do-you——

The Professor (*interrupting her*). Mildred, please! *Pianissimo!* Think of tonight!

Madam (*suddenly dropping her voice to a loud, breathy whisper*). How-do-you-do?

Mrs Fearn (*also in a loud whisper*). How-do-you (*checking herself— in her normal voice*) How-do-you-do?

The Professor. My wife is singing at a concert tonight— Shepherd's Bush—and must conserve her voice. It's most important.

Madam (*still in the loud whisper; to* Mrs Fearn). Such a nuisance, but one has to be *so* careful—especially just now, when the fogs are liable to tear one's top C to shreds.

The Professor. Or any little mental upset. Over a year ago, for instance, when we had such sad news from Tunbridge Wells— (*to* Mrs Butterworth) our dear Miss Barrett, you know—my wife lost her voice for nineteen whole days

Madam. I was distracted! I didn't know what to do!

The Professor. And then one morning I returned from some little business in town to find her carolling away like the gayest of larks.

Madam (*clasping her hands dramatically*). And, oh, the happiness of it! My very heart sang for joy.

Mrs Fearn. I'm sure. But won't you—Francie, dear——

Francie (*hastily*). Oh, yes—do please sit down, everyone— (*She glances quickly round.*) I *think* there are enough chairs.

Mrs Fearn. Of course there are, dear. Don't be silly. (*She moves to the back of the easy chair.*)

Mrs Butterworth. If there aren't, you can sit on your husband's knee! And I bet it won't be the first time this week, either —eh, Professor? (*She laughs.*)

The Professor. Now, now, for shame! You're making our little bride blush.

Madam. And, really, we mustn't intrude any longer.

Francie (*to* George). George, dear—(*She whispers to him.*)

Madam (*to the* Professor). I'm sure, dear, these good people must be wondering why we're here at all.

The Professor. Eh?

George (*moving up to the sideboard*). My—er—wife and I would be glad if you'd take a glass of wine with us.

(Madam *and the* Professor *start to utter the usual polite protestations.* Francie *moves up to* George.)

Mrs Butterworth. Go on, Madam! A drop of the right stuff inside you, and you'll sing the blessed roof off tonight! (*She sits in the easy chair.*) I shan't say No, choose how.

Madam (*giving in*). Oh, well . . . (*She crosses down* L.)

(George *and* Francie *take a bottle of wine from one of the sideboard cupboards during the following, and a tray and six glasses which* George *proceeds to fill.*)

Mrs Fearn (*to* Madam). Do sit down, won't you.

Madam. Oh—thank you. (*She sits on the sofa, and starts to unwind the scarf from about her throat, leaving it hanging loosely from her head.*)

(Mrs Fearn *sits* R. *of the table.*)

The Professor. As I should have explained (*drawing the* L. *chair a little away from the table*), knowing the house to be empty I thought it my duty to be vigilant. (*Sitting.*) And just now, while in my little garden, I fancied I heard a slight sound. My wife and I thought it prudent to investigate.

Madam (*to* Mrs Fearn). My husband has such a dread of burglars. It's really quite an obsession with him.

The Professor. My dear, robbery, and even murder, are too common these days, for us to ignore possibilities.

Mrs Butterworth. Murder? Don't speak of murder to me! It's my pet horror! (*Shudders.*) Ugh!! and as for that Jack the Ripper!

Madam (*shuddering dramatically*). Oh, don't! *Don't!*

Mrs Butterworth. Not that it was women like us he was after, though he *might* have made a mistake in the dark. Whenever I had to go out at night, I always used to hum a hymn, just to let him know I wasn't *his* sort.

Madam. As for me, the very word itself——

The Professor (*warningly*). My dear Mildred! (*A little downward gesture with his hand.*)

MADAM (*the loud whisper again*). Murder! . . . The very word itself makes me shudder!

MRS BUTTERWORTH. Same here! Even as a young girl, I could hardly sleep some nights for thinking of bodies—dead ones, of course.

(GEORGE *and* FRANCIE *come down, each with two glasses in their hands.* FRANCIE *hands one to* MADAM.)

THE PROFESSOR. Now, ladies, please, please—on such an occasion—there are less morbid topics to beguile us, I should hope.

MADAM (*accepting the glass from* FRANCIE). Oh, my dear, how kind! Thank you, indeed!

(GEORGE *hands a glass to* MRS FEARN.)

MRS FEARN (*accepting the glass*). Thank you, George.

(FRANCIE *takes a glass to* MRS BUTTERWORTH.)

THE PROFESSOR (*looking round*). This room, for instance. Very cosily arranged, I must say.

MRS FEARN. It's all quite simple, of course—just a beginning, you know.

MRS BUTTERWORTH (*taking her glass*). Eeh, thank you, luv! This is my lucky day, seemingly.

(GEORGE *and* FRANCIE *move behind the table to the* PROFESSOR.)

MADAM (*after a sip*). Very nice. Quite delicious. . . .

MRS BUTTERWORTH (*after a drink*). Bit of all right, eh! Real fruity!

FRANCIE (*to the* PROFESSOR). Will you . . .

THE PROFESSOR (*taking the glass*). Thank you, thank you. And positively your first appearance as hostess in your own house. Allow me to congratulate you.

(FRANCIE *smiles shyly and moves up to the sideboard.* GEORGE *follows her, and they take their own glasses. The* PROFESSOR *rises.*)

THE PROFESSOR (*raising his glass*). And if you will allow me, here's health and happiness to both of you.

MRS. BUTTERWORTH. Hear, hear!

FRANCIE
GEORGE } (*together; murmuring*). Thank you.

(*The* PROFESSOR *sits.* FRANCIE *and* GEORGE *cross down* R.)

MADAM. I do hope you'll both like living here. They're very good houses. We bought ours just a year ago.

(FRANCIE *sits in the armchair.* GEORGE *stands beside her.*)

MRS BUTTERWORTH (*to* FRANCIE). Your ma seems to have got some funny idea in her head about the cellar——

THE PROFESSOR (*pausing as he is about to drink*). Cellar? Why——
MADAM (*at the same time*). Really, but what——
FRANCIE. Why, is there anything wrong with it?
MRS FEARN (*hastily—reassuringly*). No, no, of course not. Just the cellar door, that's all. It—er—doesn't seem to catch properly.
THE PROFESSOR. Ah, not actually *in* the cellar itself! Our own is very satisfactory, I believe. We always refer to it as the wine cellar. It makes it seem less chill, somehow.

(*A knock is heard at the front door.*)

MADAM (*with a start and a little scream*). What's that?
THE PROFESSOR. Tut-t-t. Mildred, my love!
GEORGE (*crossing above* MRS FEARN *and putting his glass on the table*). I'll go.
(*He goes out into the passage, and off* R.)

MRS BUTTERWORTH. It'll be our Alec, come to look for me.
MADAM (*to the* PROFESSOR). Neville, your handkerchief, please. I've spilt a little wine on my dress.

(*The* PROFESSOR *rises and goes to her, taking his handkerchief from his sleeve.*)

MRS FEARN. Oh dear.
MADAM. The merest spot. The sudden rap on the door. So silly of me, but my nerves are always all keyed up before a concert. (*Taking the handkerchief.*) Thank you, my dear. (*She rubs at the spot.*)
MRS FEARN. I do hope it won't——
MRS BUTTERWORTH. Sssh! I thought I heard a voice! I bet it's Alec!

(GEORGE *returns and stands just within the doorway.*)

GEORGE. It's a man, and what d'you think? He says . . . could he go down in the cellar for a moment?
THE PROFESSOR. Eh?
FRANCIE (*at the same time*). Our cellar? But—— (*She rises.*)
GEORGE. I rather gather he used to live here at some time or other.
MRS BUTTERWORTH. Why, but it'll be Mr Meakin, for sure! That's who it is!
MRS FEARN. You'd better ask him in, George, I think.

(GEORGE *goes off* R.)

GEORGE (*off*). Will you just step inside?
MRS BUTTERWORTH. Well, just fancy that! Mr *Meakin*, of all folk! Eeh——
FRANCIE. Yes, but why should he want to——

(GEORGE *returns, followed by* MR MEAKIN. *The latter is a little man, neatly, almost dapperly dressed, carrying his hat in his hand. He has a scanty, slightly drooping moustache, and wears thick-lensed glasses that give him a goggling look of permanent surprise.* GEORGE *moves to* MRS BUTTERWORTH'S *chair.*)

MR MEAKIN (*as he enters*). Believe me—I—really—I do apologize, but—— (*He comes down* R. *of* MRS FEARN.)
THE PROFESSOR. Why, Meakin!
MR MEAKIN. Er—why, Professor—good gracious me, I never thought—how are you? (*He crosses below the table.*)
THE PROFESSOR. Well! Well! (*He holds out his hand.*)

(GEORGE *comes down* R. *to* FRANCIE.)

MR MEAKIN (*shaking hands*). An unexpected pleasure, indeed. (*He crosses to* MADAM.)—And Madam, too. (*He turns and crosses to* MRS BUTTERWORTH.) —And Mrs Butterworth! I hope you're very well.
MRS BUTTERWORTH (*displaying her glass*). Doing very nicely indeed, thanks.
THE PROFESSOR (*a wave of the hand towards* MRS FEARN). A new friend, Mrs Fearn. (*He sits* L. *of the table.*)

(MR MEAKIN *bows jerkily towards* MRS FEARN.)

(*Another wave towards* GEORGE *and* FRANCIE.) And here, my dear Meakin, are your successors—the new owners of Number Four, The Terrace!
MR MEAKIN. Ah—yes. (*A jerky bow towards* GEORGE *and* FRANCIE —*then, addressing himself to* GEORGE.) I'm afraid you'll think it all a little odd—but the fact is—I happened to be in the neighbourhood—and suddenly—quite in a flash, you know—I thought of my hammer.
GEORGE. Hammer?
MR MEAKIN (*earnestly*). Yes, yes—oh, quite a small one— (*a little gesture*) about so big—but I'd had it for years—and you know how one becomes attached to things—so I thought—as I happened to be so near, I'd call and ask you.—I should be so glad to have it back—the hammer, you know.
GEORGE. But—*we* haven't got your hammer, have we?
MR MEAKIN (*hastily*). No, no, no—please—I wasn't suggesting —not for a moment—but if you'd kindly allow me to look—I'm almost *sure* I left it there—I seem to see it in my mind's eye——
GEORGE (*increasingly puzzled*). But—where?
MR MEAKIN. In the cellar—on the long shelf—the top one, just over the gas meter—I always believe in method—a place for everything——
MRS FEARN. The cellar was white-washed a month ago, and I'm sure I never heard of any hammer being found.
MR MEAKIN. But it *might* have been missed. Workmen are so careless—the top shelf, you know.

B

GEORGE (*moving up* c., *starting to go towards the doorway—as though to settle the matter*). I'll go and have a look.

MR MEAKIN (*quickly*). No, no, indeed—I couldn't think of it— I know *just* where to lay my hand on it—that is, of course, if you'll allow me.

GEORGE. Well . . . just as you like. (*He drops down above the easy chair.*)

MR MEAKIN (*hurriedly placing his hat on the table and starting for the door*). Thank you, thank you—most kind——

MRS FEARN. But, George, it's *pitch* dark down there!

FRANCIE (*rising*). There's a candle here. (*She takes a candle-stick from the mantelshelf and moves up stage.*)

GEORGE. Here, let me—— (*He takes matches from his pocket and lights the candle.*)

MR MEAKIN. Really—all this trouble—I'm quite ashamed— but when one's had a thing for so long—you know how it is—— (*He takes the lighted candle from* GEORGE.) Ah, *thank* you—I'm so grateful—most kind——

(*With little hurried steps he hastens out into the passage, opens the cellar door and steps on to the cellar-head. Pausing there, he holds the candle aloft and peers off* R., *down into the cellar. Then he disappears off* R. *For a moment there is silence, during which they all look towards the open cellar door. Then they look at one another.*)

FRANCIE (*moving up stage and above the table; slowly—thoughtfully*). That was funny, wasn't it? . . . Just after we'd been talking about the cellar. (*She sits above the table.*)

GEORGE. And all for a tin-pot hammer! (*He shrugs his shoulders.*)

MRS FEARN. I must say, it seems a little . . . odd, don't you think? I mean . . .

MRS BUTTERWORTH. Oh, that's Mr Meakin all over! A proper old Mary Ann! I bet he's been fretting over the hammer as though it was a long-lost child!

THE PROFESSOR. Ssssh! (*After a quick glance up stage—lowering his voice.*) A nice little man, really. Most inoffensive, but, un-fortunately—h'm!—(*lowering his voice still further*) a most unhappy marriage.

MRS BUTTERWORTH. Cat and dog, I called it. And that's just what she was, too, Cora Meakin: a big, lazy, yellow cat! That's her to a tee . . . and him a scared little puppy-dog, as daren't show its nose, for fear of getting it scratched! (*She drains her glass.*)

FRANCIE. She sounds . . . awful.

MADAM. I'm afraid she was not very . . . lady-like. Loud and over-dressed, you know. Common. We didn't know her, of course; though our friend, who was living with us then, Miss Barrett, used occasionally to go to tea with her. (*To* MRS FEARN.) But then, poor Miss Barrett was old, and perhaps not quite . . . if you know what I mean. . . .

THE PROFESSOR. There's no denying, she led poor old Meakin a sad life, I fear.

MRS BUTTERWORTH. The only good she ever did him was when she died, and that's a fact!

MRS FEARN. Oh—she's dead?

MRS BUTTERWORTH. Aye. Went off to America one day, with never a word to no one. I'd never have known if I hadn't popped my head over the garden wall one Sunday morning and asked Mr M. how she was, having missed seeing her, like. "Oh, she's gone to Noo York", he says, "to visit some relations." I said summat daft about grass widows, and the next I heard she was dead! —And a good riddance, too, if you ask me, and if you'd known Cora Meakin you'd say the same.

THE PROFESSOR. And yet, in a way, I believe the little man missed her. Told me himself he couldn't bear coming back to an empty house at nights. He left and went into rooms soon after. (*He looks towards the cellar doorway.*)

MADAM. And stored his furniture. (*She looks towards the cellar doorway.*)

GEORGE. All except the hammer that he's got such a passion for. (*He comes down* R.)

FRANCIE (*also looking towards the cellar doorway*). He's a long time down there, isn't he?

GEORGE (*moving one step up stage*). I'll go and give him a shout, eh?

(MR MEAKIN *reappears on the cellar-head. Pausing there, he blows out the candle, then crosses the passage and comes back into the room.*)

MR MEAKIN. A fruitless search. Quite unavailing. (*To* GEORGE.) But thank you, all the same. I shall have to buy a new one, it seems. So many little odd jobs about a house that one wants a hammer for; and I'd set my heart on hanging a few pictures next Sunday.

MRS BUTTERWORTH. I hope you've got a landlady as looks after you. Good food and a hot brick in your bed of a night, eh?

MR MEAKIN (*a shade self-consciously*). Well, no—at least, not exactly. But then, of course, you don't know that I've—er—ventured again, so to speak.

MRS BUTTERWORTH (*speechless for a moment—staring at him*). Wha-at? You don't mean——

THE PROFESSOR. *Married again?*

MRS BUTTERWORTH. *Never!*

MR MEAKIN. About six months ago—very quietly, of course—a young lady employed by the same firm as myself.

(*A barely perceptible pause. Then:*)

MADAM (*rising and moving above the table*). Well—well, I must

say I think it *very* sensible of you, Mr Meakin. *So* much better for
you than being in rooms.

THE PROFESSOR (*recovering from his surprise*). Oh—of course. And
—and I'm sure we wish you all happiness—indeed, yes.

MRS BUTTERWORTH. And what *I* say is—better luck this time,
for I'm sure you deserve it, and that's a fact!

MR MEAKIN. Thank you. . . . Of course, I . . . can't pretend
that my poor Cora was all that I—er—could perhaps have wished
—but——

THE PROFESSOR. No, no——

MR MEAKIN. This room holds varied memories for me. . . .
But we must try to think as kindly as possible of the—er—de-
parted—must we not?

MADAM. Oh, of course we must!

MR MEAKIN (*speaking more hurriedly*). And now, if I'm to be
home before dusk, I must be getting along. It's—been a great
pleasure seeing you. Very nice indeed! Let me see, where did I
put my hat? (*He looks round, sees it, and takes it up with his left hand
from the table—the candlestick is still in his right.*) Ah—well, perhaps
we shall meet again one day. Good day to you both! Good day,
Mrs Butterworth.

THE PROFESSOR. *Good* day, Meakin. (*He rises.*)

MRS BUTTERWORTH. So long!

MADAM. You must bring your new wife to tea one day—or
perhaps a musical evening.

MR MEAKIN. Thank you. That would be a treat indeed. (*A
little bow towards* MRS FEARN.) *Good* day.

MRS FEARN. Good day. And I am so sorry about the hammer.

MR MEAKIN. Oh, please don't mention it. A trifle, I assure you.
(*To* GEORGE *and* FRANCIE.) You'll forgive me, won't you, for this
intrusion? And I hope you'll be as happy in this house as I . . .
once hoped to be. (*He gives one quick glance round the room.*) Yes. (*To
them again.*) Good day.

FRANCIE. Good day.

(MR MEAKIN, *still carrying the candlestick, starts towards the doorway.*)

GEORGE (*moving up* C. *to* L. *of* MR MEAKIN). Here, I say!

MR MEAKIN. Eh? (*Then, realizing.*) Why, God bless my soul!
how stupid of me! (*He hurries to the table and places the candle on it;
with a little tittering laugh.*) Dear, dear, what *would* people have
thought if I'd appeared with it in the street? Very droll! I must
remember to tell Lilian about it when I get home! Oh dear! Oh
dear!

(*Still tittering, he hurries up stage and off.* FRANCIE *rises and looks after
him. A few seconds later the front door is heard to close. For a moment
no one speaks. Then:*)

MRS BUTTERWORTH. *Well!* Talk about wonders never ceasing, eh?

MADAM (*rising and placing her empty glass on the table*). I must admit I'm surprised, but——

MRS BUTTERWORTH. Why, he must have took his second before Cora was fairly cold in her grave. (*She rises and puts her glass on the mantelshelf.*)

THE PROFESSOR (*somewhat tartly*). I scarcely think, Mrs Butterworth, that we need concern ourselves with the temperature of the first Mrs Meakin. After all, he has a mind and a will of his own, and he's entitled to use them.

MRS FEARN. Poor little man. I rather liked him.

FRANCIE (*suddenly—blurting out*). I didn't! I hated him! I thought he was—horrible! (*She crosses R., above MRS BUTTERWORTH.*)

MRS BUTTERWORTH (*startled*). Eh?

GEORGE. Why, Francie!

(FRANCIE *suddenly shivers, and puts her hand to her face.*)

(*Concernedly.*) What's the matter, dear? You're shivering!

MRS FEARN (*rising and moving to* FRANCIE). Francie!

FRANCIE (*uncovering her face*). I'm sorry. I'm all right now. I felt . . . cold all at once, that's all.

GEORGE. See—sit down. (*He sits her in the easy chair.*)

MRS. FEARN (*placing the footstool for* FRANCIE). She's tired after the journey, I expect.

(MRS BUTTERWORTH *moves to* FRANCIE'S R.)

MADAM (*winding the scarf round her throat*). Of course she is! We ought not to have stayed so long. Neville——

THE PROFESSOR. Yes, of course! (*He moves to the window.*) And you, Mildred, appear to be forgetting all about your concert to-night.

MADAM. Oh dear, so I am! (*She drops her voice to the loud, breathy whisper.*) Good-bye, dear Mrs Fearn. We shall meet again, quite soon, I hope.

MRS FEARN (*crossing to* MADAM). Good-bye.

MADAM (*to* GEORGE *and* FRANCIE). Good-bye, good-bye! Good-bye, Mrs Butterworth!

MRS BUTTERWORTH. Bye-bye, Madam! Be good!

THE PROFESSOR (*opening the french window*). Shut your mouth, Mildred, shut your mouth.

MADAM (*startled*). Eh? (*She comes down R.*)

(MADAM *grasps the end of her scarf, presses it over her mouth, gives a little wave of her hand, then hurries off.*)

THE PROFESSOR. The cold air, you know—striking against the back of her throat—disastrous!—Good-bye!

(*He goes, closing the french window behind him.*)

MRS BUTTERWORTH (*crossing to* C.). Aye, and it's about time

I skedaddled, too, or my young nephew'll be thinking I've run off with a black, eh? (*To* FRANCIE.) Now, don't forget them oatcakes. Hot, mind, and plenty of butter!—And if happen there's aught you want to any time, Ma Butterworth's next door.

FRANCIE (*starting to rise*). Thank you so very much.

MRS BUTTERWORTH. Nay, sit you down. I'll let myself out. (*She starts for the doorway.*) Bye-bye, Mrs Fearn. (*To* GEORGE.) Bye-bye.

GEORGE. Good-bye.

MRS FEARN. Good-bye. And I'm sure we're very grateful to you.

MRS BUTTERWORTH. Oh, go on with you! You're welcome!

(*She goes off and after a moment the front door slams.* MRS FEARN *moves below the table.*)

GEORGE (*taking* FRANCIE's *empty glass*). How d'you feel now, dear? Better?

FRANCIE. But of course. I'm perfectly all right.

(GEORGE *crosses to the sideboard and puts down the glass.*)

MRS FEARN. I can't think what came over you, bursting out like that about Mr Meakin—such a well-spoken and harmless little man, too. Whatever possessed you, dear?

FRANCIE (*not replying immediately*). It wasn't so much the man himself. . . . It was a sort of . . . feeling I had.

MRS FEARN (*looking at her—faintly puzzled*). But that's just silly, dear.

FRANCIE (*rising abruptly*). And, anyway, I don't want to talk about it! (*She crosses below the table; quickly.*) George, put the umbrella-stand up in the corner! I'm longing to see how it looks!

GEORGE. Right! (*He comes down* L., *picks up the umbrella-stand, crosses below the table and moves up* C. *with it.*)

MRS FEARN (*still looking at* FRANCIE). And what the others must have thought of you, Francie! (*She moves to her.*)

FRANCIE. What?—Oh, Mother, do stop about Mr Meakin, please! I've told you, I don't want to talk about it!

MRS FEARN (*after looking at her; quietly*). Very well, dear.

GEORGE (*dumping the stand in the corner up* L.). Phew! My word, Mother, did you carry this all the way from Notting Hill?

MRS FEARN. Of course I didn't. I took a cab. (*She crosses to the easy chair and picks up her jacket.*)

FRANCIE. But, Mother, you're staying to tea, aren't you?

MRS FEARN (*starting to put on her jacket and coming down* R.). Not today, Francie. This is your first tea in your own home. You'll like to have it by yourselves.

GEORGE (*stepping back from the stand*). How does it look?

FRANCIE. But, Mother——

GEORGE. Hey! How does it look?

FRANCIE. Lovely, dear! That's *just* the place for it!

MRS FEARN. Mind you write Auntie Edith an especially nice letter at once.

FRANCIE. Of course we will.

MRS FEARN (*going to her*). Give me a kiss, now. (*They kiss. MRS FEARN, her hands on her daughter's shoulders, looks at her closely.*) You're very happy, dear, aren't you?

(FRANCIE *nods.*)

That's right.

FRANCIE. And you'll come along tomorrow, Mother, won't you?

MRS FEARN. One day soon, anyway.

(GEORGE *is shifting the stand about an inch.*)

FRANCIE (*to* GEORGE). George, dear, mother's going.

(MRS FEARN *moves up* C.)

GEORGE. Oh. (*He moves to* MRS FEARN *and kisses her.*) Good-bye, Mother. (*He adds impulsively.*) And look here: don't worry, I'll look after her all right, I promise you.

(FRANCIE *moves down* L.C.)

MRS FEARN (*smiling at him*). You'd better.

(*She gives him a little pat on the cheek, turns and goes to the doorway. Pausing, she blows them a kiss, then goes. The front door is heard to close. There is a very short silence. Then:*)

GEORGE. Well?

(FRANCIE *looks round at him with a little smile.*)

As they say on the stage, "At last we are alone!"

FRANCIE. Yes.

(*An even shorter pause; then she takes the candlestick from the table, goes to the fireplace, and puts it on the mantelshelf.* GEORGE *crosses to her and, as she turns, catches her in his arms. They kiss.*)

GEORGE (*holding her a little away from him*). This is the beginning you know. The honeymoon was grand, but it wasn't quite real. . . . This one minute that we're living through now—this is the *real* beginning. (*In a lighter tone.*) It's a pretty solemn thought, Mrs George Briscoe.

FRANCIE (*after a happy little sigh*). I expect I'll make lots of mistakes, just at first, you know.

GEORGE. Then this is the moment for me to warn you that I have an utterly vile temper.

FRANCIE (*with a little smile*). Oh dear. I hadn't noticed it, so far.

GEORGE. That's because I've been keeping it under control, but the very first burnt rasher of bacon, and out I come in my true colours! (*They laugh, and he kisses her again.*) Darling! (*He holds her a second longer, then releases her.*) The minute's over! We've begun! (*He moves briskly towards the door.*)

FRANCIE. Where are you going?

GEORGE. Take the bags upstairs! I won't be a tick!

(*He hurries out and off* R. *The light within the room is beginning to fade just a very little, while out in the passage it is already semi-dark. She stands quite still for a moment, looking towards the doorway. Then, her head turning slowly, she looks round the room, half-wonderingly, and, somehow, one would almost fancy, half-afraid. . . . Giving herself a little shake, she takes* MRS BUTTERWORTH'S *empty glass from the mantelshelf, goes to the table, and puts it on the tray. Collecting the other glasses, she places these too on the tray, picks it up and goes briskly up stage to the doorway, on her way to the kitchen. In the doorway, she halts abruptly—and stands there—her whole figure suddenly stiff and taut. Then, with a swift movement she swings round, thrusts the tray on to the sideboard, hurries to the french window, and stands there, her back to the window, breathing quickly, the fingers of one hand pressed to her lips.* GEORGE *is heard whistling, and the next moment he returns, carrying a folded newspaper.*)

GEORGE (*as he enters*). Hello! What are you doing over there?

FRANCIE (*relaxing*). Nothing. I was just going to take the glasses into the kitchen.

GEORGE. Don't bother now. Let's have a minute by our own fireside. Come on. (*He goes to the easy chair; rubbing his hands together.*) By jove, but this is cosy, eh?

FRANCIE (*starting to cross; then pausing at* C.). George, couldn't we . . . have the gas lit . . . out there in the passage?

GEORGE. Gas? It isn't nearly dark yet.

FRANCIE. I know—but it looks so gloomy out there. Please, George.

GEORGE (*relentingly*). Oh, all right, then, just this once, as a special treat.

(*He goes up stage, into the passage, and off* R. *There is a very short pause, and then a faint glow as he strikes a match. After a moment, the glow dies down and he returns.*)

Sorry, dear, but you'll have to put up with the gloom, I'm afraid. Something wrong with the burner. I'll have a look at it to-morrow.

FRANCIE. Oh—— (*She crosses down stage to the fireplace.*)

GEORGE (*looking at her a shade anxiously; then going to her*). Francie, you are going to like this house, aren't you? You're not getting ideas into your head about it being . . . gloomy or anything?

(FRANCIE *hesitates a fraction of a second, then shakes her head.*)

Because it isn't a bit, you know, really. . . . And you'll have neighbours on either side of you, anyway. Jolly decent people, too, I should say.

FRANCIE. They do seem quite nice, don't they? . . . Not that we'll hear anything of them. I should think these walls are very thick, shouldn't you? (*She crosses to c.*)

GEORGE. Who wants to hear them, anyway?

FRANCIE (*quickly*). No—of course not, George.

GEORGE (*sitting in the easy chair, hitching his trousers*). Pots and pans rattling, babies crying, and what-not. I *like* good thick walls!

FRANCIE. But there aren't any next-door babies, dear.

GEORGE. I didn't say "next door", did I?

FRANCIE (*not seeing the implication for a moment—then, faintly*). Oh, George.

GEORGE. What?

FRANCIE (*confusedly*). Nothing.

GEORGE. Darling, will you kindly crawl out from under that gooseberry bush, and sit down.

(FRANCIE *sits in the armchair.*)

That's better. (*He opens his newspaper.*) And let me see what's been happening in the great big world.

FRANCIE. Yes, dear.

GEORGE. All I know at the moment is that this is just about the best place in it, eh?—Our own fireside.

FRANCIE (*silent for a moment—then*). I wonder if *they* ever used to sit here. . . . Mr Meakin and . . . her.

GEORGE. Eh? Oh, I expect so—when they weren't fighting.

FRANCIE. A big, lazy, yellow cat. . . . Mrs Butterworth said.

GEORGE (*turning a page of his paper*). M'm, she must have been pretty awful, I should think.

(*A short pause.*)

FRANCIE. I once read something somewhere about how houses —sort of—take on the character of the people who live in them. . . . You know—if the people have been horrible, the house itself becomes horrible, too, in time.

(GEORGE *stares at her—then bursts into a sudden laugh.*)

But it said so! I read it——

GEORGE (*still laughing*). Oh dear! I shall have to take your reading in hand, I can see.

FRANCIE (*persisting*). It said that all the hate and—nastiness soaks into the walls or something.

GEORGE. Soaks into your grandmother! Are you trying to suggest that because the Meakin couple fought and wrangled, these walls are dripping with—with hate?

(FRANCIE *is about to speak.*)

No, dear, don't say any more: just lean back and rest, and I'll read something to you. . . . (*Applying himself to his paper.*) Now let me see. . . . Ah, here we are! (*Reading.*) "On Sunday, while strolling in the grounds at Hawarden, Mr Gladstone was violently assailed by a cow, from which he only escaped by placing himself behind a tree."—There now!—(*Glancing at another column.*) "Sleeves this winter are to be worn puffed higher. . . . Bamboo furniture is all the rage. . . . The Queen last evening paid her first visit to the theatre since the death of the Prince Consort, thirty years ago. . . . Thomas Neill Cream, the poisoner, was executed at Newgate yesterday morning."

(*There is a knock at the front door.*)

Hullo!

Francie (*half-rising*). Whoever——

George (*rising*). All right. I'll go.

(*Tossing his paper on to the table, he goes out.* Francie, *who has sat down again, rises, and stands listening. The front door is heard to close, and* George *returns, followed by* Alec. *The latter is* Mrs Butterworth's *nephew: a tall, well-built young man in the early twenties, with rugged, Northcountry features. Both in speech and movement, he is somewhat slow, and his Lancashire accent is rather more pronounced than that of his aunt. In his left hand he is carrying a stable lantern, lit.*)

George (*as they enter*). Er—Francie, this is Mrs Butterworth's nephew, Alec. (*He comes above the table.*) It seems that his aunt's left a—penny behind or something.

Alec (*up* c.). Nay, a pinnie, I said. (*He points to the pinafore-apron hanging over the chair* l. *of the table.*) Yon's it, there!

Francie. Oh—of course—her pinafore!

George. Ah! (*He moves round to the chair and picks up the apron.*)

Alec. So I says to my Auntie, "I'll slip round myself and fetch it, and mebbe I'll have a word-like with 'em while I'm there."

Francie. Yes—well—I'm sure that's very nice of you. Er—won't you sit down?

Alec. Nay, I'd just as soon stand, thanks. . . . "And what's more", I says, "I'll take this here lantern, too, and then I'll be ready for owt."

George (*bewilderedly*). Yes—oh, of course.

Alec. Aye, that's how you've got to be in police force, I reckon—ready for owt.

Francie. But—are you—a policeman?

Alec (*with a nod*). Up in Burnley. . . . But what I say is—a policeman's work's never done, not even when he's on holiday. (*He stoops and sets the lantern on the floor. As he straightens himself:*) You've had Mr Meakin to see you, Auntie tells me.

George. Er—yes—why? (*He puts the apron on the table.*)

ALEC. Summat about an alleged missing hammer?

FRANCIE. He thought it was in the cellar—but it wasn't there at all.

ALEC. No. . . . (*Slowly.*) I'm wondering, you know, if he ever really expected to find it there.

(*There is a barely perceptible pause.*)

GEORGE (*looking at him—sharply*). What d'you mean?

ALEC (*bluntly*). Nowt . . . except that—if you've no objection—I'd like to take a look at that there cellar, myself.

GEORGE. Eh?——

FRANCIE. But—but why?

ALEC. Just a matter of interest, that's all.

GEORGE (*moving below the table towards* ALEC). Look here: what's all this about? Everybody seems to have got Mr Meakin and his rotten little hammer on the brain! I'm damned if I understand it!

ALEC (*calmly*). Neether do I. But there's just a chance that after taking a look at that cellar, I might.

(FRANCIE *crosses to* R. *of* GEORGE.)

But, mind you, this is unofficial. I'm acting under no authority. Just a private little investigation on my own.

FRANCIE. Investigation?

GEORGE. But what, in Heaven's name, is there in this house to investigate? There's nothing—wrong, is there?

ALEC. Not so far as I can see.

GEORGE. Then what . . . ?

ALEC. Not on the surface, that is. But who's to say as there mightn't be a deal wrong . . . *under* the surface?

FRANCIE. Under the . . .

(GEORGE *and* FRANCIE *stare at him.* FRANCIE *takes hold of* GEORGE's *hand. Then:*)

GEORGE. Would you mind telling us . . . in plain English . . . just what you mean?

ALEC. I mean it was a lucky day for Mr Meakin when his wife went off to America.

GEORGE. Well?

ALEC. And an even luckier day when she died there. What you might call a happy release—for Mr Meakin, eh?

GEORGE (*staring at him*). . . . Well?

ALEC. That's all for the moment. And now, if you don't mind, I'll just take a look at that cellar.

(*Picking up the lantern, he goes up stage and into the passage, opens the cellar door, goes through it, and off* R. *The glow from his lantern lights up the cellar-head for a moment, then dwindles and dies away as he*

descends the steps. Within the room the daylight is fading more per-
ceptibly now. GEORGE *and* FRANCIE *are standing close together, hand*
in hand, looking towards the open doorway. Then, suddenly, she re-
leases his hand, goes quickly to the fireplace, and stands there, one hand
on the mantelshelf.)

GEORGE (*crossing quickly to her*). Francie—listen, dear—there's
nothing to be afraid of! He's just a blustering Lancashire bobby,
trying to show off and be important! If he tries any more of it,
I'll send him about his business!

FRANCIE. No—no, he's right! (*Facing him now—her voice rising.*)
He's right! Don't you see? That woman—Cora—she never went
to America—she never died there—she died here, in this house!
He killed her! She's here now!——

GEORGE (*quickly*). Stop it! (*Gripping her shoulders—more quietly.*)
You're talking nonsense! I've told you—there's nothing to be
afraid of!

FRANCIE. I don't know! I don't know! I wish we'd never come
here! I hate this house! I——

GEORGE. *Francie!*

FRANCIE (*wildly*). I do! It's a wicked house, George! Wicked!
I——

GEORGE. Now, Francie, listen to me—you're just being fool-
ish——

FRANCIE (*pressing her fingers to his lips—in a loud whisper*). Sssh!
Be quiet! He's coming back!

(*A faint glow on the cellar-head grows brighter, and the next moment*
ALEC *appears.* GEORGE *has released* FRANCIE, *and they are both*
turned towards the doorway again.)

ALEC (*closing the cellar door, and entering the room*). Well, I've not
been so long, eh?

GEORGE. And have you found the precious alleged hammer?

ALEC. No, I've not . . . but I'm none so sure I haven't found
summat even more worth while than a hammer.

FRANCIE (*with a little gasp*). What?

ALEC. A rope!

FRANCIE. A—— (*She breaks off and stares at him wide-eyed.*)

(*There is a very short silence. Then:*)

GEORGE (*suddenly striding towards* ALEC; *angrily*). Look here, in
case you're too dull-witted to realize it I must tell you that you're
terrifying my wife!

ALEC (*imperturbably*). Aye, I dare say. But the females always
kick up a bit over this sort of thing. P'raps I'd better have a word
with you alone, and spare the lady's feelings.

FRANCIE (*quickly*). No—no, I want to know—please—I must
know——

ALEC. Not that there's much to tell, except that at the far end
of the cellar, the brick floor's been taken up and put down again
pretty recently. (*He rubs his chin, thoughtfully.*) Aye, about a year
ago, I'd say. (*He comes down below the table.*)

GEORGE. Well? Well, and what of it?

ALEC. Aye. That's right. What of it? *Some*body, for *some* pur-
pose, takes up them bricks, and then puts 'em down again. I
wonder why. Just what happened between the taking up and
the laying down? That, as they say, is the question!

GEORGE. There could be a hundred different answers to it!

ALEC. So there could. But only a possible one that's of any
interest to me. (*He takes the pinafore from the table.*) Eh, well, I'll be
getting back to Auntie, and think things over, eh? (*Starting to go
towards the doorway.*) I'll be seeing you later.

GEORGE. You mean, you're coming back?

ALEC (*in the doorway*). Eh? Oh aye, I'm certainly coming back.

(*He goes, and the front door is heard to close.* GEORGE *looks quickly at*
FRANCIE, *then goes to the sideboard.*)

FRANCIE. George! Where are you going? Don't leave me! (*She
hurries up to him.*)

GEORGE. I'm getting you a drink.

FRANCIE. No—please—I don't want it—I——

GEORGE (*pouring the drink*). All the same, you're going to have
it. . . . Now, don't be silly; drink this, every drop.

(*But* FRANCIE *is looking now towards the open doorway.*)

Francie! Don't look out there! Look at me, please!

(*His words do not seem to penetrate for a second, then* FRANCIE *turns and
looks at him.*)

Here—drink this.

(FRANCIE *hesitates, then takes the glass from him.*)

Go on.

(FRANCIE *drinks.*)

Again. And the whole lot this time.

(FRANCIE *drains the glass and coughing a little, gives it back to* GEORGE.)

Better?

(FRANCIE *nods.*)

More like Mrs George Briscoe, and less like a little goose?

(FRANCIE *nods again.*)

Good. (*He replaces the glass on the sideboard.*)

(FRANCIE *steals another look towards the open doorway.*)

(*He turns to her.*) And I rather *think*, my dear, we'll have that door closed. (*He crosses her moving up* C.)

FRANCIE (*grasping his sleeve*). No!—No, you're not to! Leave it open—George, please—please leave it open!——

GEORGE. But—why on earth——

FRANCIE. I don't want it closed!—I want to be able to see . . . out there! (*She crosses to the fireplace.*)

GEORGE. To—— (*He crosses down to her.*) Look here, are you proposing to spend the rest of your life staring through an open doorway?

FRANCIE. I don't want to spend any of my life in this house! I don't even want to spend tonight in it! Let's go now, George, before the night comes on! We can go home to Notting Hill, to mother!

GEORGE. And what d'you suppose she'd think? We'd be a family joke for years to come! Our first night in our new house, and acting like a couple of frightened children. For heaven's sake, darling, be reasonable!

(*Outside, in the passage a pale, thin, greenish radiance has suddenly dispelled the darkness.*)

FRANCIE (*trying to take a grip on herself*). I'm sorry. . . .

GEORGE. And what's more, you can't go home to Notting Hill. *This* is your home now. (*He moves away down* L.C.)

FRANCIE. Yes, I know. . . .

GEORGE (*turning to her*). Very well, then. Come—give me a kiss.

(FRANCIE *comes down to him and raises her face to his, and, with his hands on her shoulders, they kiss. . . . And then, looking beyond her, he sees the wanly lighted passage. Involuntarily, his grip on her shoulders tightens.*)

FRANCIE (*in a whisper*). What is it? What can you see? (*Twisting her head round, she too sees the lighted passage. Much louder.*) There's someone out there now! That light! Look!

(GEORGE *releases her and strides to the open doorway. He pauses there, then goes off* R. FRANCIE *stares towards the doorway.* GEORGE *returns.*)

GEORGE (*in the doorway; quietly*). The street lamp outside, shining through the fanlight—just that, my dear, and nothing more.

FRANCIE (*breathing a sigh of relief*). Oh. . . .

GEORGE (*coming a little farther into the room*). And that's how it is with all the rest of it. Imagination. A fool of a bobby adding two and two making five. (*He comes down to her.*) Look at me, Francie. . . . The first Mrs Meakin *did* go to America, and she *did* die there! There's nothing wrong in this house at all! D'you understand?

FRANCIE (*looking at him—after a moment—nodding her head—in little more than a whisper*). Yes, George.

GEORGE. Right! Then, for God's sake, let's forget all this nonsense. See, come and sit by the fire, and be cosy. (*With his arm round her waist, he leads her to the fire. He kneels and uses the poker.*) I'll light the gas and draw the curtains and put on those slippers you worked for me. We'll shut everything out, and be just the two of us. . . . I shouldn't be surprised if it snows later; it's cold enough outside; and in the morning there'll be frost flowers on the window-panes, and——(*He is about to light the gas when, pausing suddenly, he looks at her more closely.*) Francie, you look . . . (*Taking her hand.*) You're trembling, aren't you? (*A sudden anxious edge to his voice.*) Francie!—you're not going to faint or anything—are you?

FRANCIE. No . . . of course not, dear. . . . I'm all right . . . don't worry. . . .

GEORGE. Wait a minute! I'll open the window! (*He hurries across to the window.*) And sit down, dear, do. (*He flings open the french window.*)

From next door, faintly, but quite distinctly, comes the sound of MADAM *singing "The Last Rose of Summer". For a moment* GEORGE *and* FRANCIE *stay as they are, he by the window, she by the fireplace. And then, from the direction of the passage, there comes a tiny click as of a latch slipping. Both hear it, both look towards the passage and at the cellar door . . . which is slowly opening as—*

the CURTAIN *falls.*

ACT II

SCENE I

SCENE.—*The same. It is about ten o'clock the next morning. Snow has fallen during the night.*
When the CURTAIN *rises a few flakes of snow are still drifting down, and the branches of the plane tree are as though drawn in chalk against a grey background.* GEORGE *and* FRANCIE *are seated at the table, which is laid for breakfast.* GEORGE *is up stage of the table and* FRANCIE *is* R. *of it. It is at once evident that the atmosphere is slightly strained:* GEORGE *is wearing what may be described as a "set" look, while* FRANCIE, *whose chair is a foot or so away from the table, is looking steadily down at her hands which, lying on her lap, are plucking at a handkerchief.* GEORGE *is the first to speak.*

GEORGE. What I mean to say is, Francie, it's the principle of the thing. Begin as you mean to go on, is a pretty good motto, you know; and we certainly can't go on as *we've* begun—well, now, can we? (*She is silent.*) Eh? (*She is still silent.*) All I did was to make the perfectly reasonable suggestion that I should slip out and buy a newspaper, and I see nothing in that to make a fuss about.

FRANCIE (*not looking at him*). I didn't.

GEORGE. What?

FRANCIE (*still looking down at her hands*). I asked you not to leave me—you can't call that making a fuss.

GEORGE. Well, it was very silly, anyway. . . . It wasn't that you couldn't bear me out of your sight for two minutes—oh, no —it was because you didn't want to be left in the house alone. That was it, now, wasn't it? You didn't want to be left in the house alone.

FRANCIE (*lamely*). . . . I don't know.

GEORGE. And what *I* want to know is: what's going to happen the day after tomorrow when I start work at the office, and you're alone in the house every day?

FRANCIE (*as before*). I don't know.

GEORGE. For hours on end. . . . I don't want to sound unkind, Francie, but we can't go on like this. *Something* has got to be done about it. This—fear—whatever it is that's got hold of you—it's got to be tackled and overcome, my love.

FRANCIE (*forcing herself to look up*). Yes, George.

GEORGE. I don't believe you slept a wink last night. Twice

when I woke up, you were sitting bolt upright, and you've scarcely eaten a morsel of breakfast.

(FRANCIE *glances up stage over her shoulder—with a hint of exasperation.*)

And that's the eleventh time in—(*dragging out his watch*) exactly twenty minutes that you've looked at that door. I've timed you.

FRANCIE (*faintly*). Is it?

GEORGE. And, anyway, I've got a theory about that door. (*As he replaces his watch.*) I remember when we lived in Hammersmith, every time we slammed the front door, the clock in the back sitting-room used to stop dead.

FRANCIE (*looking at him*). But, George, what's that got to do with . . .

GEORGE. My theory is, that every time anyone steps on a certain board in this room, it causes that door to open. You often get things like that in fairly old houses.

FRANCIE (*unconvincedly*). Do you?

GEORGE. Yes, you do. . . . And another thing: that buzzing bluebottle of a policeman from next door, said he'd be coming back. Well, he hasn't.

FRANCIE. No.

GEORGE. No. Because he's been thinking things over, and even he, dim as he is, has begun to realize that it's all—bunk!

FRANCIE. Do you—do you really think so, George?

GEORGE. I've thought so all along—*and* said so! Bunk! (*Pushing his chair back and rising*). I wouldn't exchange this house for Buckingham Palace! (*Firmly.*) I mean that, Francie.

FRANCIE. Yes, George.

GEORGE. It isn't everybody who's given a house for a wedding present. Most people'd be jumping for joy; not inventing a lot of bogie nonsense about it. And just look: you haven't even drunk your tea!

(FRANCIE *takes her cup, sips, and gives a little shudder.*)

FRANCIE. It's cold.

GEORGE. Of course it is, by now. (*He strolls towards the window.*) Snow seems to have stopped, anyway.

(*He stands by the window, looking out. There is a pause.* FRANCIE *pours her cold tea into the slop-basin, rises, and starts to collect the crockery together. After a moment, she leaves these, goes round above the table and stands there, looking towards* GEORGE.)

FRANCIE. George.

(GEORGE *turns round.*)

George, I'm sorry I was so silly just now. Do please go out and buy your newspaper, if you want to, dear.

α

GEORGE. It isn't that I particularly *want* a newspaper. It's just that . . .

FRANCIE. Yes, I know. I shall be perfectly all right. . . . I've got to get used to being alone, I mustn't be silly.

GEORGE. Half the time, I bet, you'll be so busy about the house, you'll scarcely notice I'm not here.

FRANCIE. No. *(She shakes her head and moves towards* GEORGE.) I shall never be too busy for that, George.

GEORGE *(starting to go to her)*. You know—you do say the nicest things, Francie, sometimes.

FRANCIE. I think them all the time . . . about you.

GEORGE. Darling. *(He kisses her.)* The shop's only a few yards away. I'll be back in no time. I needn't even shut the front door.

FRANCIE. Don't hurry.

(GEORGE *kisses her again, then goes up* C.)

GEORGE *(in the doorway)*. Two minutes.

(He blows her a kiss, then goes out. FRANCIE *remains quite still for a moment, facing up stage; then she turns to the table, picks up the cruet and takes it to the sideboard. Instead of returning immediately to the table, she pauses up* L., *and looks round the room. Her gaze travels slowly the length of the* L. *wall, then the invisible, or audience wall, then, much more quickly, the* R. *wall, until, with a little half-turn, she is looking at the doorway. From where she is standing, she cannot see across the passage. Almost holding her breath, she tiptoes a little more out into the room, until the cellar door is within her vision. Seeing that it is closed, she relaxes, giving herself a little shake, as though telling herself not to be such a fool, starts to go to the table, but changes her mind and goes to the fireplace. Kneeling, she takes a little hearth brush and commences to flick it over the hearth. Her back is to the doorway, so that she does not see the figure which suddenly, and without the slightest sound, appears there—*MR MEAKIN! *He is wearing an over-coat, and is carrying his hat in one hand, and a small leather bag in the other. Seeing* FRANCIE, *he pauses a moment, then gives a gentle little cough. Scrambling to her feet, she swings round, sees him, and drops the brush into the hearth.)*

FRANCIE *(checking a scream—her voice sharp-edged with fear)*. Mr. Meakin! What are you. . . . What d'you want here?

MR MEAKIN *(obviously startled by her reactions)*. Oh, please—do forgive me—I've startled you—so stupid of me—but you see, I quite forgot—I just walked in—but I assure you, I . . . *(He has started to advance a little into the room.)*

FRANCIE *(backing down* R.). No! No! Don't come near me—go away! George is upstairs! I shall call him!——

MR MEAKIN *(very disturbed)*. But, my dear young lady—if you'd only let me explain—I hadn't the least intention of——

(GEORGE *enters up* C., *paper in hand.)*

Ah!

GEORGE (*surprised*). Mr. Meakin! Why, what on earth—— (*He hurries down between them to* FRANCIE.) Francie, what's the matter?

FRANCIE (*clinging to* GEORGE). He frightened me, George! He —he crept in and frightened me!

GEORGE (*sharply*). What? (*He releases himself and moves towards* MR MEAKIN.) Now, look here—what's all this about, eh?

MR MEAKIN (*hastily; very perturbed*). But I assure you, I did not creep—no, really—these goloshes I am wearing, they make no sound—I should never dream of creeping—never——

GEORGE. Yes, but what are you doing here at all, I'd like to know?

MR MEAKIN. Why—why, as yesterday, I chanced to be in the neighbourhood, on some transaction for my firm, The Falcon Insurance Company. And it occurred to me to wonder if you'd made your insurance arrangements for this house, so I thought I'd just pop a little of our reading matter into my bag—er—and leave it with you—just a matter of business. . . .

GEORGE (*very directly*). But d'you usually walk straight into a house and scare the womenfolk, Mr Meakin?

MR MEAKIN (*hastily*). No, no—indeed—really, I'm quite ashamed—but you see—your front door was standing wide open —and through sheer force of habit, I walked in—instinctively, mechanically, you know—without thinking—having lived for so many years in this house. . . . I can assure you, I couldn't have been more startled and distressed when I realized what I'd done.

GEORGE (*looking at him*). I see. (*Then, after a moment he crosses below the table. Reassured, but still somewhat brusquely.*) That's all right then. We'll say no more about it.

MR MEAKIN. Thank you. (*To* FRANCIE.) I *do* hope you've quite recovered from your fright. Believe me, I wouldn't have had it happen for the world. (*To* GEORGE.) No, really!

GEORGE (*as* FRANCIE *does not immediately reply*). Francie?

FRANCIE (*a trifle unsteadily*). I'm all right now, thank you.

MR MEAKIN (*coming down stage, putting his hat on the chair R. of the table and opening his bag; to* GEORGE). I'm afraid, after my stupidity, you'll scarcely feel inclined—but if you *would* allow me to leave these few papers—a most reliable firm—of the highest possible integrity. (*Taking a few papers from his bag, he places them on the table.*)

GEORGE (*off-handedly*). Thanks. I'll have a look at them some time.

MR MEAKIN. Perhaps this morning—I mustn't press you, of course—but if you *could*—I shall be passing again this afternoon on my way home—and any little point that you might wish to have explained—— (*He moves down right to* R. *of* GEORGE.)

GEORGE (*as before*). All right, I'll see.

MR MEAKIN. Thank you, thank you, most kind of you, I'm

sure. (*To* FRANCIE.) And as for our little misadventure just now, I shall not forgive myself in a hurry, but—all's well that ends well, shall we say? (*A little bow to her.*) Good day. (*He picks up his hat; to* GEORGE.) *Good* day.

(*With noiseless footsteps, he hurries up* C. *towards the doorway; then, suddenly, as though arrested by something on the floor by the doorway, he halts. For no more than a few seconds he stares down, even bending his head very slightly; then, recovering himself, he hurries off, and the front door is heard to close.*)

FRANCIE (*relaxing*). Oh dear! What a fright he gave me! I never heard a sound. He seemed to just . . . rise up out of the floor.

GEORGE. Still, I suppose it is an easy thing to do, when you've lived in a house so long, going in and out through that front door countless times. . . .

FRANCIE. But he's so—when he went out, just now—did you notice?—As though he suddenly . . . saw something (*pointing*) on the floor—there—by the door!

GEORGE. Eh? (*He goes up to the doorway, and looks down at the floor. He looks a little closer, then, straightening himself, he moves the door-mat an inch or so with his foot. He crosses towards the window.*) There's nothing there, anyway, nothing at all.

FRANCIE (*moving to the table*). All the same, George, I do think there's something—odd about him. (*She moves above the table.*)

GEORGE (*with rather forced lightness*). My dear Francie, there's something just a little odd about most of us. Some people might think it a little eccentric of us to have the breakfast-things still on the table at nearly midday.

FRANCIE. I know—it's disgraceful! (*Bustlingly, she starts to pile the crockery.*) I mustn't let it be like this other mornings, must I? Where's the tray? Oh, I know—in the kitchen!

(*She hurries up stage, out into the passage, and off* L. GEORGE, *by the window, listens for a moment, goes very quickly to the doorway, drops on to one knee, lifts one end of the little mat, and peers under it. As he does so,* MADAM *appears at the french window, and, immediately behind her, the* PROFESSOR. *Peering through the window, she taps at the glass. At the sound,* GEORGE *drops the mat, and springs to his feet with a little smothered exclamation. Then, seeing her, he starts to go towards the window.*)

MADAM (*opening the window a little*). May we come in?

GEORGE (*above the table*). Oh—yes—please do.

MADAM (*opening the window wider and kicking her boots against the step outside to remove the snow*). And how are you this cold and frosty morning? (*As she enters; over her shoulder to the* PROFESSOR.) Don't bring any snow on to this pretty carpet, Neville! (*To* GEORGE.) Do forgive us, won't you? We're just going out, and I have a little present for your wife—these roses. (*She moves in to* L. *of the table.*)

(MADAM *is quite attractively dressed for out of doors. A long fur stole is wrapped round her throat, and she is carrying a little muff in one hand, and three or four white roses in the other. The* PROFESSOR *is wearing a black coat and is carrying his hat. Before entering, he, too, kicks his boots against the step.*)

GEORGE. She's in the kitchen. (*Starting for the doorway.*) I'll call her.

MADAM. No, no, don't. Please! We can't stay a minute!

THE PROFESSOR (*entering*). Good morning, good morning. (*He drops down* L.)

MADAM. See, I'll put them on the sideboard. Tell her to give the poor darlings a little drink of water, will you? They'll be so thirsty.

GEORGE. I think she's coming now. (*He crosses to* R. *above the easy chair.*)

(FRANCIE *enters up* C. *from off* L., *carrying a tray.*)

FRANCIE (*with a little exclamation of surprise*). Oh——

MADAM. My dear, this is an unearthly hour to pop in, but we shan't stay a minute.

THE PROFESSOR (*who appears to be in a somewhat testy humour*). Our clocks must be all wrong, Mildred. Look—they've barely finished breakfast.

FRANCIE. Oh, no, we finished hours ago. We've been talking. I'm so ashamed——

MADAM (*dropping her muff on the sofa*). Nonsense! See, I just wanted to leave you these few roses. White. So bridal, I thought. I felt you simply must have them. (*She moves up* L.)

FRANCIE (*leaning the tray by the sideboard and taking the roses*). Oh, but how kind of you! Thank you! Roses in November! (*She smells them.*) Lovely, lovely things!

MADAM. They're from the bouquet I had at the concert last night. A present from the Committee. Wasn't it nice of them?

THE PROFESSOR. Why? Seeing that you sang without fee, it was the least they could do.

MADAM. Now, Neville!

THE PROFESSOR (*impatiently*). Well!

MADAM (*to* FRANCIE). I'm afraid my husband's a very cross man this morning. It's the weather, you know.

THE PROFESSOR. Beastly snow! Beastly east wind! Beastly Nature at her very beastliest! (*To* GEORGE.) Eh?

(FRANCIE *crosses to the fireplace and takes a little vase from the mantel-shelf.*)

GEORGE. Oh, I don't know——

THE PROFESSOR. Well, I do! It does disgusting, indescribable things to my liver! (*He shudders.*) Brrrrh! !

MADAM. Now, dear, I'm sure we don't want to hear *anything* about your liver.

THE PROFESSOR. Why not? You're everlastingly singing about your heart! Either it's broken or it's jumping for joy or something. Surely I can put in a word for my liver!

(FRANCIE *moves up* C. *with the vase.*)

MADAM. Really, Neville! (*To* FRANCIE.) These husbands! Oh dear!

FRANCIE (*to* GEORGE). George, will you take this into the kitchen and fill it with water, please?

(GEORGE *takes the vase and goes out up* C.)

MADAM (*to* FRANCIE). And are you beginning to feel more settled in? (*She moves* C. *towards* FRANCIE.)

FRANCIE (*hesitating*). Well—of course—a new house is always a little—strange just at first, I suppose.

THE PROFESSOR (*moving about*). A month or so, and you'll feel you've never lived anywhere else. Fine houses, these. Solid. Substantial. I wouldn't part with mine to the Widow of Windsor herself. There's nothing like owning your own house. Gives you a feeling of security. The day I was able to buy mine was the happiest of my life!

MADAM. Just a year ago today. Neville and I are having a little celebration tonight. Dinner in town, and a theatre.

FRANCIE. How very nice.

MADAM. Oh, and I've treated myself to a new evening gown, and I'm so excited! It's to arrive this afternoon!—Tell me, may I slip it on, and pop in and let you see it? I'd *so* like your opinion!

FRANCIE. Oh, please—I'd love to see it—though I don't think my opinion can be of much use.

THE PROFESSOR. There's only one opinion that any woman ever has of another woman's dress—"Of *course*, it looks *awful* on her!"

(GEORGE *enters with the vase.*)

MADAM (*with rather forced raillery*). Now, Neville, dear, that will do: even an east wind is no excuse for cheap cynicism.

(*There is a knock at the front door.* GEORGE *puts the vase on the sideboard and goes out.*)

MADAM (*during this—to* FRANCIE). And don't forget, dear, you're both to spend an evening with us quite soon. Do you play Whist?

FRANCIE (*crossing to the sideboard*). Well. . . . I'm not very good at it.

MADAM. Never mind. I expect we're dreadfully out of practice. I don't believe we've touched a card since our friend Miss Barrett left us—have we, Neville?

THE PROFESSOR (*craning his head forward—peering short-sightedly at a picture—absently*). M'm? Miss Barrett what?

MADAM. Poor dear, she'd an absolute mania for cards. Night after night, until all hours. (*She moves to* R.C.) And of course she played so *very* badly—her mind, you know—she couldn't concentrate. I'm sure there were times I felt I never wanted to see a card again.

THE PROFESSOR (*still peering at the picture*). Oh, by the way, did you have a visit from our old friend Meakin just now? We *thought* we saw him go by.

FRANCIE (*arranging the flowers in the vase*). Yes . . . yes, he did just call in.

MADAM (*with a faint smile*). Really? (*She moves to the fireplace.*) Not another cellar-hunt for the missing hammer?

FRANCIE (*forcing a smile—shaking her head*). No—no, not the hammer this time.

THE PROFESSOR (*turning from the picture*). Ah. (*Moving towards the window.*) We just wondered. Are you quite ready, Mildred?

(*Before* MADAM *can reply*, GEORGE *enters. He is accompanied by* MRS FEARN. *The latter, who is of course wearing outdoor clothes, is looking just a little worried and distrait.*)

FRANCIE (*surprised*). Why, Mother!

MRS FEARN (*a little anxious edge to her voice*). Francie, dear . . . (*Seeing the others—breaking off.*) Oh—oh, good morning. (*She comes* R.C.)

(GEORGE *moves to the easy chair.*)

MADAM. Good morning. We've been paying an early call upon our newlyweds.

THE PROFESSOR (*opening the window*). And we're just leaving. This is our weekly shopping morning. A ghastly ritual! (*Looking out.*) Ha! I thought as much! The wind's dropped, and there's a fog coming on!

MADAM (*turning quickly towards the window*). Fog! Oh, *no*!

MRS FEARN. Oh, but it was quite thick in places as I came along.

THE PROFESSOR (*stepping just outside the window and putting on his hat*). Come on, Mildred—look sharp, for heaven's sake—and let's get the shopping done!

(*He turns up his coat collar, and goes off.*)

MADAM (*snatching up her muff*). Oh! Oh, this cruel, wicked climate! Why do we live in it? (*To* FRANCIE.) This afternoon, don't forget—a private view of my new dress! (*To* MRS FEARN.) Good-bye!

MRS FEARN. Good-bye.

MADAM (*with a wave of her muff towards* GEORGE). Good-bye. (*Hurry-*

ing to the window.) Neville! Neville, you rude, ungallant man,
where are your manners? Wait for me, please!

(*Holding the muff to her mouth, she steps out of the window, and hurries
off.* MRS FEARN *and* FRANCIE *move down* R.)

GEORGE. Who's she to talk about manners, anyway! Leaving
the window wide open! (*He crosses above the table to the french window, and closes it.*)

FRANCIE (*to* MRS FEARN—*speaking through* GEORGE's *last words*).
Mother—what a lovely surprise—we didn't expect you!

MRS FEARN. . . . No.

GEORGE (*by the window*). By jove, but he was right. It's going
to be a genuine, hundred-per-cent pea-souper, a real old London
Particular.

(*The light has already begun to lose some of its strength. From this point
it grows more and more dim as the fog thickens. Outside, beyond the
window the day begins to take on a faintly leaden-greenish tinge, which
deepens, as though the world is approaching some rather frightening zero
hour.*)

FRANCIE (*sensing something in her mother's tone and manner*). Mother
—you look—what's the matter?

(GEORGE *turns from the window, goes to the table and picks up the
papers which* MR MEAKIN *has left.*)

MRS FEARN (*after a barely perceptible pause*). I'm a silly old
woman, I suppose . . . but I had to come . . . I couldn't rest,
Francie, until I'd . . . satisfied myself.

FRANCIE. But—what about?

MRS FEARN (*not immediately replying; going to the chair* R. *of the
table and sitting*). When I got back to Notting Hill last night—I
don't know what came over me—I seemed all—I couldn't settle
down to anything—I kept telling myself I was a fool, but that
didn't do any good. I *couldn't* get it out of my mind.

GEORGE (*behind the table*). But—get *what* out of your mind?

MRS FEARN (*turning a little in her chair to look up stage*). Out there
—that door.

GEORGE. Eh? (*He puts the papers down again on the table.*)

FRANCIE (*at the same time*). The door!

MRS FEARN. Opening and closing . . . and no one there. It
seemed such an absurd thing to—to have on one's mind: just a
door (*a little descriptive gesture with one hand*), opening and closing.

FRANCIE. But it does! We've seen it, haven't we, George? It
does, Mother!

MRS FEARN (*quietly*). I know. I saw it myself—yesterday—
several times.

GEORGE (*with rather forced matter-of-factness*). Well, it's shut now, anyway. And what's more, Mother, I'm surprised at you, getting all worked up about a door with a faulty catch.

MRS FEARN. I was rather surprised at myself, George. And a little bit angry. It seemed so silly. But there it was. . . . And there was nothing else for it but to come along, and—and just *see* you both. That was it—I felt I had to *see* you!

GEORGE. Well, I may as well tell you, you're not the only one this morning with a bee in your bonnet. Francie's got a tidy-sized one in her's, too—*and* about the selfsame door. The best thing we can do is take a few tables and chairs and camp out on Hampstead Heath. Cut doors right out of our lives!

FRANCIE. It isn't the door itself! You know it isn't! It's—what —might be——

GEORGE. Beyond it? A flight of very ordinary stone steps, darling, leading down to a very ordinary cellar—just that!

MRS FEARN. Yes, George. (*She rises.*) To look at! And it still would be, even if little Mr Meakin *had* killed his wife and buried her down there.

FRANCIE (*sharply*). Mother! (*A sharp little intake of breath.*)

MRS FEARN (*turning and crossing to the fireplace*). I saw Mrs Butterworth in the High Street just now, and she told me of this—this idea that you've all got in your heads.

GEORGE. I hope your "all" doesn't include me. (*He crosses to* L. *of* FRANCIE.) You mean to tell me, you really believe that little Meakin's a murderer, and that . . .

MRS FEARN (*after a second's hesitation*). No, I don't. All the same, this—horrible idea's there, and it's got to be got rid of. Francie can't go on living in this house, with thoughts like that in her head. A week from now, and she'll be afraid of her own shadow.

GEORGE (*hesitating—pacing a little way up stage, then turning—giving in*). All right, then: we'll send for the budding Chief Constable, next door, and let him get busy with his bucket and spade.

MRS FEARN. You needn't bother to send for him. He's coming, anyway. He's hunting about the neighbourhood, trying to borrow a pick-axe and things.

GEORGE. Good. (*He starts to stroll towards the window, hands in trousers pockets.*) All I ask, then, is that having ripped up our cellar floor, and no rotting bones having transpired, he'll kindly put it back exactly as he found it. After which, we'll all have a hearty good laugh over the whole thing.

FRANCIE. I know you think I'm being very silly, George, and I'm sorry. But I'm not the only one——

GEORGE (*going towards* FRANCIE). Now, listen: let's forget all about this, for a while! Let's talk about something else—*please!*

MRS FEARN (*briskly*). You're quite right, George. Let's concentrate on something "real". (*Indicating the table.*) That, for instance.

What is it? An early lunch, or a very late breakfast? (*She sits in the easy chair.*)

FRANCIE (*quickly*). I know. I'm ashamed. Where's the tray, George?

GEORGE (*fetching the tray from by the sideboard*). Here—I'll get it!

FRANCIE. You'll stay to lunch, Mother, won't you? (*To* GEORGE, *as he returns with the tray.*) No, George. I'll clear. (*She takes the tray from him, and sets it down on the table.*)

MRS FEARN. I'm not sure, Francie, I'll see. Can I help you, dear?

FRANCIE. No, Mother. (*Picking up the insurance papers and* GEORGE's *newspaper.*) Put these somewhere, George, please.

(GEORGE *takes them from her.*)

How very dark it's getting. (*She starts to pile the breakfast things quickly on to the tray.*)

GEORGE (*going to the sideboard*). It's the fog. Just look at it, out there.

FRANCIE (*busy with the crockery*). You'd almost think it was the night arriving too soon, wouldn't you?

GEORGE (*tossing the insurance papers on to the sideboard, but retaining the newspaper*). Thank goodness I don't have to be out in it, anyway.

FRANCIE. Poor mother's got to get back to Notting Hill, don't forget.

GEORGE (*moving down* L., *opening his newspaper*). Oh, well, it'll probably lift pretty soon. You never know.

MRS FEARN. Don't worry about me, children. I'll be all right. I wouldn't think much of myself as a Londoner, if I were afraid of a wisp of fog.

(GEORGE *sits on the sofa, and opens his newspaper. There is a short pause, during which* FRANCIE *completes her task.*)

MRS FEARN. Anything in the paper, George?

GEORGE (*scanning it*). Not a thing.

MRS FEARN. Just a plain blank sheet, I suppose.

GEORGE. Eh? . . . M'm. . . . There's quite a bit here about the Neill Cream hanging. . . . "Passed a restless, uneasy night, tossing from side to side, and moaning. . . . He rose at six, looking bloodless and haggard, his eyes staring, his face and hands twitching convulsively. Billington was the executioner, and the length of the drop was five feet."

MRS FEARN (*breaking in*). George! In the circumstances, is that quite the happiest item you can find to read to us?

GEORGE (*hastily*). Oh, sorry! (*He turns hurriedly to another page.*) Ah! Here we are—"Pedestrians in a North London suburb yester-

day afternoon were considerably dismayed at hearing violent
and abusive language hurled at them apparently from the house-
tops. Some time elapsed before the offender was discovered to be
a parrot. The bird is believed to have recently escaped from a
nearby vicarage."

MRS FEARN. That's *much* better.

(FRANCIE *moves up* c. *with the tray.*)

(She rises.) All right, dear; I'll see to the cloth.

(A pause. GEORGE *is studying his newspaper.* FRANCIE *goes out, carrying
the tray.* MRS FEARN *goes to the table, takes off the cloth, and commences
to fold it, quickly at first, then more slowly, her eyes fixed on the seated
figure of* GEORGE. *Finally, she puts the folded cloth down on the table,
and comes quietly down stage towards him, pausing before she quite
reaches him. Absorbed in his paper, he is not at first aware of her. Then,
looking up, he meets her eyes.)*

GEORGE. What's the matter?

MRS FEARN. That's just what *I* was going to ask *you*, George.

GEORGE *(not speaking for a moment—laying the paper down beside
him).* What d'you mean?

MRS FEARN. You know, it's very right and proper of you to
spare Francie's feelings. But there's no need to spare mine. *(He is
silent.)* Just now, more than once, the thought crossed my mind
that you were bluffing—bluffing for all you were worth.

GEORGE *(shifting his position slightly; non-committally.)* Oh?

MRS FEARN *(a step nearer to him).* Now, George, I want you to
tell me: at the back of your mind is there even the tiniest suspicion
that there *may* be something wrong—here?

GEORGE *(opening his mouth to speak—obviously going to bluff then
changing his mind).* You know . . . if you'd asked me that an hour
ago, I'd have wanted to laugh at you.

MRS FEARN. But now?

GEORGE. I'm not so sure—or rather, I'm not *quite* so sure as I
was. *(A pause. He rises and glances towards the door. He moves below
the table.)* Little Meakin was here, just now.

MRS FEARN. Here?

GEORGE. Something about insurance.

MRS FEARN. . . . Well?

GEORGE *(facing her—going nearer to her).* Mind—you're not to
breathe a word of this to Francie. Her nerves are quite enough on
edge, as it is.

MRS FEARN. I'm not quite a fool. . . . What did the little
Meakin man do, or say, that . . . ?

GEORGE. He—*looked*—he just *looked*—for no more than a
second—at something on the floor, up there by the door. And
I'd a pretty strong feeling that he didn't at all like what he saw.

(Mrs Fearn *looks at* George *for a second or two, then she turns and goes up stage to the doorway. Bending a little, she looks at the floor.*)

Under the mat.

(Mrs Fearn *moves the mat a little with her foot, and bends down lower. For an appreciable moment she remains thus; then, slowly, she straightens herself, and replaces the mat with her foot.*)

Mrs Fearn. Blood?

George. Ssssh! (*A quick gesture, indicating that* Francie *in the kitchen may overhear. He moves* c.)

Mrs Fearn (*coming down stage to* George; *dropping her voice*). What d'you think . . . ?

George (*after a shrug*). All I know is, he saw it, and he didn't like it. (*More slowly.*) It—it *meant* something to him. I'd almost swear it did.

Mrs Fearn. He didn't—say anything?

George. Eh? (*Lightly sarcastic.*) Oh, yes, of course. He said, "This blood-stain happened the night I killed my wife, Cora, and dragged her body, step by step, down into the cellar."

Mrs Fearn. That isn't so very funny, George.

George (*a shade impatiently*). Of course he didn't say anything! The whole thing happened in a flash. The next second he was bowing and scraping himself out of the door. For all I knew at the time, I might have imagined it.

Mrs Fearn. But you didn't.

George. I didn't imagine that stain, did I?

(Mrs Fearn *looks at* George, *and is about to speak. Then, checking herself, she crosses* R., *below the fireplace. A fairly long pause. Outside, the fog has thickened considerably, and the room has grown increasingly dim and shadow-haunted.* George *goes to the window.*)

Thicker than ever. Just look at it! The whole length and breadth of London blotted out!

Mrs Fearn (*not looking at him*). I don't want to look at it. I want that man—policeman, or whatever he is—to come quickly and—and let's get at the truth of all this! However ugly it may be—let's know the truth! (*Just a shade louder, and with the faintest hint of ebbing self-control.*) That's what *I* want, George!

George (*turning from the window and crossing to her*). Let me tell you what *I* want. I want you to be brave and very calm—for Francie's sake . . . *whatever* may be *in store.* . . . You understand?

Mrs Fearn (*calmly again*). Yes, George, of course. I'll try.

(*She is about to put her hand on his arm, but, at a slight sound from off stage, she quickly withdraws it, moves to the armchair down* R. *and sits.* George *moves away below the table. The next moment,* Francie *enters. She comes in hurriedly, as though controlling an impulse to run, and comes down* c.)

GEORGE (*meeting her as she comes down*). Francie! What are you hurrying for? Is anything wrong?

FRANCIE (*shakily*). No—but—it's so dark out there—you can hardly see across the kitchen—I *couldn't* stay there another minute!—I *couldn't*!

GEORGE (*taking her hand and leading her to the fireplace*). Silly! See —come and sit down.

FRANCIE. And then—I thought I heard a noise somewhere! (*She glances fearfully towards the doorway.*)

MRS FEARN (*exchanging a swift look with* GEORGE). Oh, nonsense, dear. What sort of a noise?

FRANCIE. I don't know. A sort of queer . . . thud.

GEORGE (*banteringly*). Sort of thud! (*To* MRS FEARN; *in the same tone.*) Why didn't you tell me your daughter had noises in the head? I'd never have married her.

FRANCIE (*with a little helpless half-laugh*). Oh, George!

(*Somewhat reassured, she is about to sit in the easy chair. At that moment there is a faint but quite definite sound from off stage. It is, in fact, precisely as* FRANCIE *has described: a sort of hollow thud.*)

FRANCIE (*stiffening*). *There!*—That's it! Did you hear it?

(*A very short pause, while they listen.*)

GEORGE (*unconvincingly*). A fog signal on the railway line.

FRANCIE. There's no railway near here. And it isn't outside at all! It's *in* the house! I know it is!

MRS FEARN. Francie——

FRANCIE. But it is!—It's in the cellar! There's something moving about down there!

GEORGE (*holding her*). Francie! Listen, please! There's nothing to be afraid of, d'you hear? I'll go all over the house myself— now—every nook and corner—I'll settle this, once and for all——

FRANCIE (*clinging to him*). No, don't! George, you're not to! No!

MRS FEARN (*rising*). Hush! Hush, both of you! Be quiet, will you! (*She moves to* L. *of* FRANCIE.)

(*They pause for a second and listen. And now, from across the passage, comes a quite unmistakable sound: the clump-clump of slow, heavy footsteps.*)

FRANCIE (*her voice mounting with fear*). There's something— coming up from the cellar! (*Louder still.*) It's coming up from the cellar!

GEORGE (*thrusting her from him almost roughly—starting towards the doorway*). Stay where you are! Both of you! Don't move!

FRANCIE (*hysterically*). Where are you going? No! Come back! George!

(Upon her last word there is a loud rat-tat on the cellar door, and the next moment it is flung open. The figure of a man, lit by the somewhat bizarre light of the stable-lamp he is carrying, is seen standing on the cellar-head. It is ALEC. FRANCIE'S speech has ended in a little scream. The positions now are: FRANCIE R., by the fireplace; MRS FEARN a little above her, and slightly to L. of her; GEORGE a few paces from the doorway, and a little to R. of it.)

ALEC (*as the others gasp and stare; cheerfully*). Anybody home? It's only me, Alec, you know, from next door. (*Taking in the situation.*) Hope I haven't scared you folk, eh?

FRANCIE (*faintly*). Oh—— (*She sits in the armchair down R.*)

GEORGE (*recovering; bursting out*). What—what the devil are you doing there, man? What game d'you think you're playing? The demon king in a pantomime, or what?

ALEC (*considerably abashed; venturing into the passage*). Eeh dear, now, hark at that! Someone's blundered, and, seemingly, it's me, eh? (*He closes the cellar door behind him.*)

GEORGE (*fuming*). Of all the damn-fool, loutish tricks! (*He turns abruptly away, and crosses to* FRANCIE.)

MRS FEARN (*quickly; quietly*). George, please——

GEORGE. Francie—are you all right?

FRANCIE (*a little shakily*). Yes—yes——

ALEC (*in the doorway now; contritely*). I'm sure I beg the ladies' pardon. I'd no thought in coming up through cellar but to save trailing slush in your lobby. If there was one thing my mam were down on, it were trailing slush in the lobby. In through the back door and off with your clogs—eether that or a clout on your bottom that'd set the crockery ringing? - -

MRS FEARN (*hastily*). Yes, of course, Mr.—er——

ALEC. And my mam's bite were worse than her bark—and that were bad enough, as the school inspector found to his cost. "My Alec's seven year old," she says, "and I'm keeping him home with the croup," she says, "but at that, he's a better man or you," she says, "with the pimples on the back of your neck and the pink cotton-wool in your ears, so out of my lobby, afore you get this wet mop in your face." (*A reminiscent chuckle.*) He went, all right.

GEORGE. Very interesting. (*He moves below the table.*) But I'd be even more interested to know just how you got into that cellar. (*He moves up L. of the table to* ALEC.)

ALEC. Why, through backyard door, of course, and down the steps coalman uses.

MRS FEARN. But, surely, there's a door there, and it's locked. (*She sits in the easy chair.*)

ALEC (*advancing about two paces into the room and setting the lamp down on the floor immediately in front of him*). Aye. But I thought happen Auntie's key'd fit, *and* it did—so here I am, with my pick-

axe and crowbar and spade down there, all ready to get to work.
(*Dropping his voice into a more confidential tone.*) But see here: there's
one thing we must understand: all this is what they call sub rosie:
I'm acting under no official authority; just a private little investigation of my own, so to speak.　　　. . .

GEORGE. Don't you think we'd be wiser to do the thing properly
right from the start, go to the police station now, and tell them
the facts?

ALEC. What facts?

(*The others are silent.* GEORGE *makes a little half-helpless, half-im-
patient gesture.*)

Nay, if you've a mind to go to police station, then all right, and
I'm game to go with you; but don't go kidding yourself we've
aught in the way of facts, because we haven't. For aught we
know, Cora Meakin may be over in America, alive and well, this
minute, and playing Yankee Doodle on a penny whistle. Same
with little old Meakin: when he went down yon cellar yesterday,
he may have been a murderer returning to the scene of his crime,
like they say they do, or that hammer yarn of his may be as
genuine and open as Blackpool sands. We don't know. All *we've*
got is suspicion. Sus-picion! And it's like yon fog out there. Sooner
or later it'll lift, and then . . . I reckon we'll see what we shall see
—eh?

(*A very short silence. The cellar door opens. The upstage part of the room
is now fairly well lit by the glow of the stable-lamp at* ALEC's *feet.
He himself is thrown into rather dramatic relief against the darkness
of the doorway and passage behind him. The rest of the room is very
shadowy, while the window itself is no more than a large patch of green-
grey dimness.*)

MRS FEARN (*trying to keep her voice steady but not quite succeeding*).
I'd like you to tell me, d'you think your*self* that you're going to
—find anything—down there? I mean, do you your*self*. . . .

GEORGE (*starting impatiently*). Mother, how can he possibly . . .
(*He breaks off.*)

FRANCIE (*quite quietly*). He will. I know he will.

GEORGE. Darling, you don't know anything of the sort. You've
worked yourself up into the state when you're ready to believe
anything—if only it's bad enough.

(FRANCIE *does not reply, but turns towards the fireplace.*)

ALEC (*to* MRS FEARN). You've asked me a question, ma'am,
and I'm going to tell you summat as I'd keep to myself if I were
back in Burnley: the folk there'd think me daft—and mebbe I
am. It's this: when I were down in that cellar just now, a sort of
—I dunno—feeling came over me, as though I were very—welcome there.

Mrs Fearn. Welcome?

(Francie *turns from the fireplace, rises and looks at* Alec.)

Alec (*haltingly*). Like as if summat—were glad someone'd—turned up at last. . . .

George (*moving to* L. *of* Alec). Look here: are you trying to make out now that the place is haunted, or what?

Alec. Ghosts, d'you mean? Me? Not me! I've no belief in such flummery! (*And then, haltingly again.*) I didn't say I saw or heard aught, did I? A sort of feeling, I said. . . .

Francie. That something was glad!

Alec. And mebbe it was only me that was glad—to be in a nice dry cellar, out of the fog and slush, eh? Aye, I reckon that's more like it. (*A barely perceptible pause. He stoops and picks up the lantern.*) And any road, I'm doing no good cackling here: I'd best be getting on with the job. (*He turns to face the passage—his back to the room—starts to go out, then halts abruptly. He raises the lamp a little higher.*)

Mrs Fearn (*dropping her voice almost to a whisper*). What's the matter?

Alec (*his back still to the room*). Naught . . . 'cept that I could have sworn I shut that door.

(*The cellar door is wide open.* Mrs Fearn *rises. There is a quite short but well-marked pause. Then after a shrug of his shoulders,* Alec *crosses the passage, and goes on to the cellar-head. For a moment, he stands there, his lantern raised, looking down into the cellar.*)

Alec (*looking towards the room; with a laconic nod*). Oh, well . . . so long, you folks.

(*He goes off* R. *into the cellar, his shadow wavering for a moment on the back wall of the cellar-head, the glow from his lamp dying away as he descends the cellar steps. There is a very brief pause, during which the three stand quite still. No movement whatever. The latest incident of the open door is of course in their minds, but with one accord they are silent. Then, at precisely the same moment, each makes a move.* George *goes up* C. *to the room door and closes it very quietly.* Francie *crosses to the french windows, and stands there.* Mrs Fearn *moves to the armchair below the fireplace, hesitates as though about to sit, but remains standing. From this point, until just before the fall of the* Curtain, *all moves should be made as soundlessly as possible, and voices should be just a shade lower than normal.*)

George (*his back to the door; forcing a natural tone*). You know, something tells me that, by this time tomorrow, we'll be laughing ourselves hoarse over all this . . . feeling a bit ashamed, too, at having been such fools.

Mrs Fearn (*after a second's pause—as though his words did not immediately penetrate; quietly*). Yes, George.

(GEORGE *seems about to say something further, but abandons the attempt.*)

FRANCIE (*by the window; her back to the room*). You can't even see the other houses now. Not the faintest trace. Everything's gone. . . . I think fog's frightening . . . as though only just this room, and the things you can actually see and touch are real . . . with nothing left out there, but a great big—blank.

MRS FEARN (*moving to the chair R. of the table and sitting; matter-of-factly*). If you like to slip on your things, and step out of the front door, you'll find the world's still struggling on, fog or no fog.

(GEORGE *crosses to the fireplace.*)

FRANCIE (*turning from the window*). It's just the—the feeling it gives me.

MRS FEARN (*dryly*). A few years ago, dear, I'd have been wondering if I oughtn't to give you a nice Gregory powder. What are you doing, George?

GEORGE (*taking matches from the mantelshelf*). Lighting the gas.

MRS FEARN. Very sensible. Francie, do, for heaven's sake, sit down! You make me feel all jumpy. Why don't you do some sewing or something?

(GEORGE *proceeds to light the gas brackets on either side of the fireplace.*)

FRANCIE. I think perhaps I'll do a little darning.

MRS FEARN. I certainly should. It'll take your mind off things.

(FRANCIE *moves up to the sideboard and takes from one of the cupboards a work-basket with socks and darning materials.*)

GEORGE (*having lit the gas*). There, that's it!

FRANCIE. I should think the type of woman who really likes darning, can't have any mind at all, shouldn't you?

(GEORGE *crosses to the windows and proceeds to draw the curtains.*)

MRS FEARN. I don't know. I quite like it, myself. It's soothing. (*To* GEORGE.) Thank you, George. That's better. Shut it right out.

(FRANCIE *comes down to the chair L. of the table and sits. She places the basket on the table.* GEORGE, *after a moment, moves a little above* FRANCIE's *chair, and stands there, hands in trousers pockets.* FRANCIE *takes some socks from the basket.*)

FRANCIE (*commencing to darn*). I wonder what . . .

MRS FEARN. Yes?

FRANCIE. I was going to say, I wonder what—he's doing now, down there. I can't hear a sound.

MRS FEARN (*firmly*). I'm not listening for sounds. Push that basket over here, please.

D

(FRANCIE *pushes the basket to* MRS FEARN.)

Is there any spare wool? Ah, yes.

(*A very brief pause.* MRS FEARN *starts to thread a darning-needle.*)

FRANCIE (*a shade louder—as though to distract her own thoughts*). What's happened to that lovely tie I worked for you, George? You haven't worn it lately.

GEORGE (*somewhat absently—as though he too is listening for sounds*). The green and yellow one? I don't know. It's somewhere knocking about, I suppose. (*His voice trails off, as he turns his head and looks towards the doorway.*)

MRS FEARN. George has been married over a week. He is no longer colour-blind . . . are you, George? (*As* GEORGE *does not reply, she looks up, sees the direction of his gaze, gives a little frown, and applies herself with increased concentration to her needle-threading.*)

FRANCIE (*her eyes on her darning*). He said it was the loveliest tie he'd ever seen, when I gave it to him—didn't you, George?

GEORGE (*still looking towards the door; quite softly*). Ssh!

From somewhere beneath the house there comes a sound, muffled, rhythmic, and remote: a pick-axe striking against a brick floor. The three within the gas-lit room neither speak nor move. They sit, very still and tense, not looking at one another, listening to that distant, hollow thud . . . thud . . . thud, as—

the CURTAIN *falls.*

SCENE 2

The CURTAIN *remains down in complete darkness for a few moments, during which the thudding sound is still heard, louder at first, then growing fainter, and finally dying away.*

When the CURTAIN *rises some time has elapsed.* GEORGE *is now standing by the french window, parting the curtains a little and peering through the chink.* MRS FEARN *is still seated* R. *of the table, but has turned her chair, so that she is now facing the audience.* FRANCIE *has not moved, save that she is now sitting with her hands loosely clasped on the table in front of her. Beside her are an ink-stand, pen, and a sheet of note-paper. In the middle of the table are the work-basket and the darned socks. For an appreciable moment, nobody speaks. One feels, in fact, that nobody has spoken for a quite considerable time. And then:*

MRS FEARN. Have you written it yet? What have you said?

FRANCIE (*not stirring for a moment—then picking up the note-paper and reading*). "Dear Auntie: George and I are simply delighted with the perfectly lovely umbrella-stand you have sent us. We shall always treasure it." (*She pauses.*)

MRS FEARN. Well, go on? (*She changes her position slightly.*)

FRANCIE. That's all . . . so far.

(MRS FEARN *shrugs expressively.*)

Well, I don't seem able to *think* of anything. (*Not changing her position.*) George, you might help. What else can I say to Auntie Edith?

GEORGE (*still looking through the chink*). Why not tell her we're nicely settled in, and busy digging for bodies in the cellar?

MRS FEARN. Don't be silly, George, please!

FRANCIE (*dropping the paper and pushing it from her*). It's no use! I'll have to leave it till tomorrow! I can't do it now!

(MRS FEARN *is about to speak, but checks herself. There is a very short pause.*)

MRS FEARN. Is the fog beginning to lift at all, George?

GEORGE (*not turning—shaking his head*). It looks just as though someone had hung a dirty grey blanket right outside the window.

MRS FEARN (*dryly*). How nice. I don't wonder you can't tear yourself away from it.

GEORGE. . . . What?

(*Another moment, then, closing the chink, he moves away from the window, to behind* FRANCIE's *chair. A further very short pause. Then* MRS FEARN *utters a short exclamation and suddenly rises.*)

FRANCIE. What's the matter, Mother?

MRS FEARN (*moving to the fireplace*). Nothing. Pins and needles in my leg. I must move about. (*She paces to and fro, in front of the fireplace.*)

FRANCIE. We seem to have been sitting here for hours. How long is it since he—went down there?

GEORGE. Heaven knows!

FRANCIE. Thank goodness that horrible noise has stopped! It seemed to beat right into one's brain, didn't it? It made me feel . . . awful.

GEORGE. It's quiet enough now, anyway. Not a sound. (*He pauses, looks towards the door, then suddenly starts to go towards it.*)

MRS FEARN (*ceasing to pace; up* R.C.). What are you doing now? Where are you going?

GEORGE (*halting abruptly; lamely*). Nowhere. I just thought I'd . . .

(*He hesitates. His eyes meet* FRANCIE's, *and, as though reading her thoughts, he starts again for the door, opens it, and goes out into the passage. He pauses again there, as though listening.* FRANCIE *rises, and starts to go up* L. *Moving very quietly, making no sound whatever,*

GEORGE *goes on to the cellar-head.* FRANCIE *halts, half-way to the door, and somewhat to* L. *of it. The cellar-head is in almost pitch darkness, but there is a very faint light coming from the lamp below, so that* GEORGE'S *face can be just dimly seen, as he bends forwards and a little downwards, trying to see into the cellar.*)

MRS FEARN. Can you see anything, George?
FRANCIE. Ssh! Be quiet, Mother!
MRS FEARN (*impatiently*). My dear Francie, there's no need whatever to act as though we've lost our voices! We might just as well behave quite normally, and not like silly, frightened children!

(GEORGE *turns and, still moving very quietly, comes back a little way into the room.*)

MRS FEARN (*to him*). What are you creeping about like that for, George? Really, I declare, you're as bad as Francie!
GEORGE. Sorry. . . . The steps turn at the bottom. I can't see anything. I thought I could hear him moving about, though. I'm not sure.
MRS FEARN (*moving to the fireplace*). Well, shut the door. And do, for heaven's sake, let's stop fidgetting about! (*She sits in the easy chair.*)

(GEORGE *closes the door, then starts to cross towards the fireplace. Before he quite reaches it,* FRANCIE *crosses to him.*)

FRANCIE (*speaking with sudden earnestness*). George—I want you to promise me—whether there's anything—or nothing—we won't stay here in this house, will we?
GEORGE. But, darling—surely—if everything's all right——
FRANCIE. No—no, whatever happens—we *can't* live here! I believe I'd go mad! I mean that, George!
MRS FEARN (*before* GEORGE *can speak*). Oh, Francie, how can you be so silly? As houses go, it's a very good house indeed!
FRANCIE (*intensely*). It isn't! It's a—bad house! I've hated it from the moment I set foot in it! There's something—wrong about it? Can't you—can't you feel it yourselves?
GEORGE. No, I can't! And what's more, I haven't forgotten the first time we saw the place: you were all excitement and enthusiasm.
FRANCIE. I pretended I was! I had to! It was a present from your uncle!
GEORGE (*gently*). You're all wrought up, darling, aren't you? Never mind. You'll feel quite differently tomorrow, see if you don't. The fog'll be gone, the sun'll be shining, and everything will be—different.

(*He puts his hand on* FRANCIE'S *shoulder. She looks at him in silence for a moment, then shakes her head, and moves away from him, below the table.)*

FRANCIE (*facing front now; more quietly*). It's like that house I used to pass by on the way to school. I used to run by on the other side of the road, and try not to look at it. . . . Black with dirt, and windows all jagged glass, and no leaves ever grew on the tree at the front—you know the place I mean, Mother.

MRS FEARN. It had got a bad name for some reason or other —I forget what—drains, probably.

FRANCIE. Folk used to say that lights floated about the rooms at night, and just before dawn a harp could be heard playing in a room right at the top. . . . The haunted house, they called it. (*She ceases speaking abruptly, a shade self-consciously, and looks quietly towards MRS FEARN; then starts to move down L.*)

GEORGE (*half-scoffingly, but quite gently and kindly*). Lights? Harps? Haunted houses? Oh dear, Francie, whatever next?

(*He starts to go to her. As he does so, the lights in the room suddenly sink down to about one quarter pressure, until only a small blue flame remains in the two globes, to cast a thin bluish twilight over the room. FRANCIE gives a little scream, GEORGE a startled exclamation. MRS FEARN springs to her feet.*)

And *now* what the hell's up?

FRANCIE			George? What is it? What's happening now?
MRS FEARN	(*together*).		What on earth's going on in this house? My goodness me! What . . .

GEORGE (*loudly*). That great clumsy fool down there—he must be messing about with the gas——

MRS FEARN (*agitatedly*). He's probably split a gas pipe or something! George, don't stand there! *Do something at once!* (*She moves quickly up C.*)

GEORGE (*striding to the door*). All right—wait a minute——(*He flings open the door and dashes out into the passage; shouting.*) Hey, what the devil d'you think you're playing at down there? What have you done to the gas?

(*A muffled, quite unintelligible voice replies from below.*)

GEORGE (*shouting*). The gas, you damn fool, *the gas!* (*Then starting to come back; dropping his voice.*) He's coming up!

FRANCIE (*sinking down on to the sofa*). Oh!——

(*The glow from the stable-lamp is reflected on the cellar-head as ALEC starts to come up the steps.*)

MRS FEARN (*crossing hurriedly to* FRANCIE). Francie—are you all right? (*She looks up stage.*) What's he doing? Why is he so slow?

(*The reflection on the cellar-head slowly brightens. Then ALEC appears.*)

GEORGE (R. *of the door; as soon as* ALEC *appears*). What in God's name are you up to, man? We're groping about in the dark up here! (*He breaks off, checked by something in* ALEC's *manner.*)

ALEC (*coming out into the passage; his tone is strangely subdued*). Eh? Oh, aye—I caught my sleeve on the mains-tap just now. I reckon I must have turned it a bit, like.

GEORGE (*with less assurance*). Well—well, for goodness sake, go and turn it back at once.

(*But* ALEC *makes no move to do so. Instead, he comes slowly and in silence into the room. The lamp in his hand casts a circle of light. The others stare at him.* FRANCIE *rises. There is an appreciable pause. Nobody speaks. Then:*)

(*Moving to* ALEC—*pausing before quite reaching him; in a hushed, awed tone.*) What's the matter?

ALEC (*looking at* GEORGE *for a moment; then, quietly, and with no dramatic emphasis*). Murder.

(*There is a quick intake of breath from* MRS FEARN, *followed by a moment of stunned silence. Then:*)

MRS FEARN (*in little more than a whisper*). No! . . . No! . . .

(ALEC *looks at* MRS FEARN *without speaking. Then he turns to* GEORGE.)

ALEC. No more nor a two-three inches down. . . . Wrapped in —stuff.

GEORGE (*quickly*). No—no, don't tell us any more—just now! (*He hurries across to* FRANCIE.) Francie—are you all right?

(MRS FEARN *turns to* FRANCIE *and puts her arm round her.*)

FRANCIE (*her voice surprisingly calm and steady*). Yes. . . . Yes, I'm quite all right.

GEORGE (*in front of her; anxiously*). See, darling, sit down a moment.

FRANCIE (*as before; gently disengaging herself from* MRS FEARN *and crossing her to* GEORGE). I don't want to sit down. Please don't worry, George. . . . Now that we really know—and don't have to —imagine things any more—I'm all right.

(GEORGE *looks at* FRANCIE *a bit doubtfully.* MRS FEARN *sinks down upon the sofa.*)

MRS FEARN (*to* ALEC). You are *sure!* There's no *mistake!*

ALEC. Not in *my* mind—and the cellar's there; for anyone as likes to take a look.

MRS FEARN. No! Oh, *no* . . . ! It's awful, George—*awful*—that little man—here in this very room, for all we know—and then— dragging her—— (*She breaks off and presses her hands to her face.*)

GEORGE. Let's try not to think of that part of it, Mother.

(Mrs Fearn, *her hands still to her face, shudders.*)

Francie (*not emotionally*). He's such a very ordinary little man to look at—isn't he?

Alec. As for little or tall, the only one as need bother about that now'll be the hangman.

Mrs Fearn (*muffled from behind her hands*). Oh . . . !

Alec. There's summat else I've found. (*From his jacket pocket he takes a little object and tosses it on to the table.*)

(George *and* Francie *go to the table,* George *down* L. *of the table,* Francie R. *of it.*)

Francie. An ear-ring . . . a crescent moon and star of little blue stones.

Alec. It must have caught in the flannel stuff he used for wrapping. If Meakin stood one chance in a million, *that*'d dish it for him! (*He moves away* R.)

Francie (*bending over it*). Cora Meakin's. . . . Big and showy . . . just like she must have been!

(*She stretches out her hand to touch it.* George *grasps her wrist and gently draws it back.*)

George (*quietly*). No—don't touch it!

Alec (*moving to the table and picking up the ear-ring*). See, I'll put it on mantelshelf. (*He crosses to the fireplace and puts the ear-ring on the mantelshelf, behind one of the ornaments.*)

Mrs Fearn (*rising; with more control, but still a sharp nervous edge to her voice*). Listen—you two—you must pack a few things straight away and come to Notting Hill. George, see to that at once—you can't stay here now.

Alec (*moving* C.; *before* George *can react*). Here, hold hard a bit. Before we do any flitting, this has got to be reported to the proper quarters.

George (*with forced lightness*). What do we do? Go out and find the nearest policeman and tell him we've got a body in our cellar? (*He crosses to the fireplace.*)

Alec. No, sir! We act in a proper manner, and our first stop's the police station!

Francie. George! (*She crosses to him.*)

Mrs Fearn (*breaking in; her voice still sharp-edged*). Can't anything be done about these lights? This gloom's making things worse!

Alec (*starting for the doorway*). Aye, I'll just pop down and turn on yon tap.

Mrs Fearn (*flinching at the thought*). Down there!

Alec (*in the doorway*). And why not? There's only one man need be feared now of what's down there—and his name's Meakin!

(*Immediately there is a loud rap on the front door. For a second nobody moves. Then:*)

GEORGE. And there's just a chance—that may *be* Meakin—he was to call for some papers!

ALEC (*reacting immediately*). Right! Stay here, you folk! I'll see to this!

(*He goes off,* R.)

MRS FEARN (*with shuddering apprehension*). Supposing it is him—Meakin!—What shall we *do?*—What'll *happen?*

GEORGE (*listening*). Hush!

(*Voices can be heard off stage.*)

FRANCIE. It isn't! It's . . .

(MRS BUTTERWORTH's *voice is heard off stage. The next moment she appears in the passage. She is dressed for out of doors, and is in a state of considerable excitement.*)

MRS BUTTERWORTH (*as she appears; calling back to* ALEC). Don't shut that door, Alec! There's someone out there! (*Bustling into the room and stopping short.*) What the heck's going on here? Blind man's buff? What's wrong with your lights?

(ALEC *reappears in the passage, goes on to the cellar-head, and off down the steps.* MRS BUTTERWORTH *advances two or three more steps.*)

MRS BUTTERWORTH. Well? Are you all struck dumb, or what?

MRS FEARN (*in a very controlled voice*). We're in great distress, Mrs Butterworth. Something very dreadful . . .

MRS BUTTERWORTH (*more subdued*). Ah?

MRS FEARN. That woman—who lived here—Cora Meakin——

GEORGE. She didn't go to America—she never went away from this house—she's down in the cellar *now*—all that's left of her!

(*For one long moment* MRS BUTTERWORTH *stares. Then, she gives one quick nod of her head, turns, and hurries out into the passage.*)

MRS BUTTERWORTH (*calling off* R. *and beckoning*). Come in here, luv, come in! Look sharp! I want you!

(*She returns into the room. As she does so, the lights come up.*)

MRS BUTTERWORTH. Out in the fog just now—I bumped slap-bang into someone I reckon you'll be very interested to meet! And here the lady is! Mrs——

(*She breaks off, as* MRS DUBINSKI *appears in the passage. She is about forty, of somewhat over-generous build, and flashily dressed: loud colours, any amount of obviously imitation jewellery and a hat with a thick veil.*)

Mrs Butterworth (L. *of the door*). Mrs—What did you say your name was?

Mrs Dubinski (R. *of* Mrs Butterworth; *scarcely audible*). Mrs Dubinski.

Mrs Butterworth (*encouragingly*). Lift your veil! Come on! Let's hear you proper!

(*After a second's hesitation, the woman lifts her veil, revealing a florid, carelessly made-up face.*)

Mrs Dubinski (*louder—with a toss of her head, and a touch of bravado now*). Mrs Len Dubinski!

Mrs Butterworth. Ah! But what was it when *I* knew you, luv?

Mrs Dubinski (*again after a second's hesitation, and again dropping her voice*). Cora Meakin.

Mrs Butterworth (*dramatically—with a sweeping gesture towards the figure in the doorway*). Cora Meakin!

The Curtain *falls.*

ACT III

SCENE.—*The same. It is about two minutes later.*

When the CURTAIN *rises* ALEC *is standing up stage, his back to the door, which is closed;* MRS DUBINSKI *is seated on the chair* R. *of the table, the chair being turned to face the audience;* MRS BUTTERWORTH *is standing beside her, a little to* R. *of her;* MRS FEARN *is seated in a very tense and upright attitude on the sofa.* GEORGE *is standing* L., *his back to the curtained french window;* FRANCIE *is seated in the armchair, down* R. MRS DUBINSKI *is ill at ease: her eyes wander restlessly about the room, she plucks nervously at the material of her dress, varying this by fingering her lips or touching the brim of her hat.*

MRS BUTTERWORTH (*who is just finishing unwinding a lengthy scarf from round her throat; still rather breathlessly*). Cora Meakin!—You could have knocked me down with a feather! Of all folk in the world! Cora Meakin! (*She tosses the scarf on to the easy chair.*) It was a—a what's it called?—what's the word for it?

MRS FEARN (*impatiently; on edge*). Oh, never mind! Never mind the word!

MRS BUTTERWORTH (*to* GEORGE). Here, you—you've been to school—what's it when you drop your ring in the sea, and next day you're filleting a bit of fish, and there's your ring in its gullet.

GEORGE. Coincidence?

MRS BUTTERWORTH. Coincidence! That's it! There's me, groping along the Cromwell Road, scarce able to see my hand in front of me, when I have a collision with a lady who says, "Pardon me" in a voice I know as well as my own. "Cora Meakin", I says, "or I'll eat my hat!" (*Triumphantly—with a show-man's gesture.*) And there she sits, as large as life, the last person you ever expected to see, I'll bet my boots!

MRS DUBINSKI (*momentarily screwing up her courage; protesting shrilly*). Oh, you will, will you? Then, when you've done betting your boots and eating your hat—which couldn't taste worse than it looks—perhaps you'll kindly inform me just why you've dragged me here! (*Struggling to her feet; even more shrilly.*) Why've you brought me to this house, and who are these folk, and what are they staring at me for, like a lot of stuffed dummies? (*To* MRS FEARN.) You! D'you take me for a Barnum and Bailey freak or something?

MRS BUTTERWORTH (*soothingly*). Now, luv——

MRS DUBINSKI (*turning on* MRS BUTTERWORTH; *stridently*). And as for you, you as good as kidnapped me! (*As* MRS BUTTERWORTH *opens her mouth to speak; louder still.*) Oh, yes, you did! You could see I wasn't quite myself, and you took advantage of it. (*Not quite so loudly.*) I'd had a drop of gin, if you must know, to keep out the fog, and—and it had upset me! (*Louder again.*) But I'm all right again now! And I'm not stopping here! It's come over me all at once, I don't like this room—no, nor the company in it! (*She turns as if to hurry up stage.*)

MRS BUTTERWORTH (*grasping her arm*). Here—not so fast!

MRS DUBINSKI (*wrenching her arm free*). Let go, will you! You've no right. . . . (*She hurries determinedly up stage—then stops dead, in front of* ALEC, *who, stolid and imperturbable is standing directly in front of the door.*) Oh! And what may you be, eh! Doorkeeper at Buckingham Palace? Just you step aside, young man, and let me out of this house, d'you hear?

(MRS BUTTERWORTH *moves to the fireplace.* ALEC *does not move.* MRS DUBINSKI *makes a futile effort to thrust past him. He holds her off, not roughly, but quite effortlessly.*)

ALEC		Here, hold hard a bit! That'll do, now!
MRS DUBINSKI	(*together*).	Here, you keep your hand off, will you!
MRS FEARN		(*Springing to her feet; still on edge.*) Oh, why—why are we wasting time? Why don't we go for the police at once? The police!

(*A split second of silence. Then:*)

MRS DUBINSKI (*upon whom the word "police" has had an instantaneous and electrifying effect—swinging round*). The police! Police, did you say? (*She comes down* C.)

(ALEC *looks at* MRS DUBINSKI *quickly.*)

MRS FEARN (*moving above the table*). We know now, don't we—whoever it is down there—it isn't . . . .

ALEC (*with a quick warning gesture*). Ssh, will you! "Hear all and say nowt" is the motto for just now. (*He moves a little away from the door and indicates* MRS DUBINSKI; *more slowly.*) Yon's the tongue I'd like to hear do a bit of wagging! I've a fancy it could be very interesting if it had a mind (*he moves a step nearer to her*), eh?

(MRS DUBINSKI *stares at him, then makes a convulsive movement, as though to try another dash for the door.*)

(*Instantly, his hand is on her arm.*) Nay, steady now, let's have no more rough and tumble. Somebody might get hurt.

MRS BUTTERWORTH (*hurrying to* MRS DUBINSKI *and taking her other arm; coaxingly*). Now, see here, luv, you come with me and sit you down. (*She leads her slowly down* L.) You know me, don't you? I'll see you're all right. We were good neighbours in the old days, eh? (*Talking to distract her.*) Eeh, and what a one for borrowing you was, to be sure! You never let me have that little enamelled saucepan back, you know—but never mind. . . . That gin's got you all on edge, the nasty stuff! What you need's a bit of a sit-down on this lovely sofa here. Put you right in no time. (*She almost forces her down upon the sofa.*) There! That's better, eh?

(*She sits down stage of* MRS DUBINSKI, *still with her hand on the latter's arm. Since the rise of the curtain,* FRANCIE *has sat perfectly still, listening. Now, she rises, and, very quietly and unobtrusively, crosses up* C. *to the sideboard, where, still so quietly as to attract no attention, she proceeds to pour out a glass of wine.* MRS FEARN *moves to* L. *of the table, and then round to the back of it.* GEORGE *relaxes his attitude and moves a little away from the window.* ALEC *comes down* R.C.)

MRS DUBINSKI (*still manifestly ill at ease*). But—why've they got the lights on, and the curtains drawn, in the middle of the day?

GEORGE. Because of the fog. It was dark as night in here.

MRS BUTTERWORTH. It was beginning to lift a bit as we come in. (*To* MRS DUBINSKI; *reassuringly.*) You see, luv, there's naught to be afraid of at all.

MRS DUBINSKI (*as before*). I don't like it—no—and I don't know why you've brought me here—and just look at my hat, all on one side—oh dear. (*She tries fumblingly to straighten her hat.*)

ALEC (*moving in to* C.; *with the air of one about to take charge of affairs*). Never mind about your hat. You'll have time enough to titivate when I've done with you.

MRS DUBINSKI (*staring at him*). Eh?

ALEC (*directly in front of the sofa*). I've three questions to ask you—and you're going to sit there till they're answered, choose what!

MRS DUBINSKI (*her agitation increasing*). I—I don't know what you're talking about, young man, or what right you've got to question me! I'm a free agent, I'd have you know!

ALEC. You're a dead body, you mean.

MRS DUBINSKI. *What?*

ALEC (*pointing at her; accusingly*). You went to America over a year ago, and died there! So how is it you're sitting there, large as life, instead of mouldering in your grave? Question number one!

MRS DUBINSKI (*trying to rise; restrained by* MRS BUTTERWORTH). Now, see here, I'll thank you to——

ALEC (*holding up his hand to silence her; louder*). Question number two: why're you in such an almighty sweat to get out of this house? (*He moves a step nearer to her. She recoils slightly.*) Whose ghost is it you're scared you may see? And what way's it most likely to come, down through the ceiling, or (*with terrific significance*) *up from the cellar?*

MRS DUBINSKI. You're talking riddles! Riddles! (*To* MRS BUTTERWORTH.) He is! I don't know what he . . . (*To* ALEC.) What are you getting at?

ALEC (*as before*). Question number three: why did you nearly jump out of your skin just now when the word "police" was mentioned?

MRS DUBINSKI (*struggling to her feet; blusteringly*). That'll do! Ghosts and police! I've had enough! You'll be telling me next I'm wanted for something—murder, maybe! (*She crosses to* ALEC.)

ALEC (*looking at her very narrowly; in a much quieter tone*). Mebbe.

(*A sudden complete silence.* MRS DUBINSKI *stares at* ALEC *with parted lips and dropped jaw.*)

MRS DUBINSKI (*in little more than a whisper*). *Murder?*

ALEC (*still quietly*). It was you who said the word first. . . . But if you don't like it, we'll think of another—bigamy, for instance.

MRS DUBINSKI (*catching at her breath; still staring*). . . . *Bigamy!*

ALEC. That's the name for it here, when a lawfully wedded couple carry on the game you and little Meakin are playing. Here's you alive and kicking, and him with a new wife. . . .

MRS DUBINSKI (*genuinely surprised*). What? You mean to tell me, Henry's gone and——

ALEC. A new wife—and bold as brass about it!

MRS DUBINSKI. Ha! That pasty-faced typist woman, I bet!

ALEC. Her face'll be red enough when she finds she's no more Mrs Meakin than I am! And you! Who the heck's *Mr* Dubinski when he's at home, I'd like to know!

MRS DUBINSKI (*with a flash of spirit*). The same as when he's out of it! And if he were in this room this minute, he'd as soon knock your teeth down your throat as look at you!

ALEC. You'd better look out for yourself, then! When he finds he's been cherishing another man's legal wife, he mayn't be too pleased!

MRS DUBINSKI (*off her guard; heatedly*). Don't you worry about Len Dubinski! I'm as much his legal wife today, as I was when I married him twenty years ago!

MRS BUTTERWORTH (*rising*). Cora Meakin! How can you stand there and . . .

MRS DUBINSKI (*even more off her guard*). And don't Cora Meakin me, neither! I'm not, and I never was, Cora Meakin—so there!

MRS BUTTERWORTH. What?

MRS DUBINSKI. I . . . (*Checking herself.*) Oh! (*She realizes that she has blundered. Her voice snaps off. Her expression changes. She sits R. of the table.*)

MRS BUTTERWORTH. Are you trying to . . .

ALEC (*never taking his eyes off* MRS DUBINSKI). Shut up, Auntie. (*To* MRS DUBINSKI; *quietly.*) Go on.

MRS DUBINSKI (*not speaking for a moment—then, in a weakened voice*). You make me—say things.

(*She turns a little away, and finds herself face to face with* FRANCIE, *who, wine-glass in hand, has come quietly down stage.*)

FRANCIE (*offering the glass*). I thought perhaps you'd like . . .

MRS BUTTERWORTH. On top of all that gin? She'll be tiddly! (*She sits* L. *of the table.*)

(MRS DUBINSKI *looks at* FRANCIE, *then at the glass. She hesitates, then puts out her hand and takes it.* FRANCIE *sits above the table.*)

MRS FEARN (*coming down* L. *to the sofa; very tactfully—or so she imagines*). See, come and sit over her with me, dear, and tell *me* what the trouble is.

MRS DUBINSKI (*looking at her—after taking a sip from her glass*). I'm sure I don't know who *you* are, Madam, but you look and talk like a missionary worker! (*Another drink, half-draining the glass.*) And as for my troubles—all right! All *right*! (*She breaks off and turns quickly to* ALEC; *with a sudden sort of jaunty recklessness.*) I may as well be hung for a sheep as a lamb—and you're determined to hang *someone* before the day's out, I can tell by the look on your face!

ALEC (*dourly*). Never mind about my face!

MRS DUBINSKI. I don't. And if I was twenty years younger, I still wouldn't. (*She drains her glass and gives it back to* FRANCIE.) Ta, dear. Very nice, if you're partial to invalid port. (*She rises and moves towards* ALEC. *She pauses a moment before speaking, as though for dramatic effect.*) I was just twenty-one when I married Mr Dubinski . . . and from that day to this, I've never stopped being married to him! Henry Meakin was—what's the word?—an interlude.

MRS BUTTERWORTH. H'm! It isn't the word we'd use in Burnley!

MRS DUBINSKI. Oh, he thought he'd married me on the level, did little Henry. . . . You see, after me and Mr Dubinski'd been married about ten years, his nervous system went all to pieces and he was ordered a complete rest—very complete—on Dartmoor.

MRS FEARN. Not—prison?

MRS DUBINSKI. With me left to struggle along on my own!

ALEC (*taking a step nearer to her*). Your idea of a struggle being to pose as a single woman and fool a decent, hard-working little man into a sham marriage!

MRS DUBINSKI (*defiantly*). You can hand me one medal, anyway: I *meant* to play fair! I was all for a quiet home life, and knowing where my next meal was coming from. I was even prepared to cook it. I did, too, for a bit. I kept this house so you could have eaten your dinner off the floor—until the day dawned when you'd have had to if you'd wanted any, for that's where I chucked it, the whole damn lot!

MRS BUTTERWORTH. And if Henry Meakin had been a Burnley man, he'd have chucked you alongside it, (*grimly*) aye, he would and all.

MRS DUBINSKI. That'd have been better than looking at me the way he did, like an old tom-cat with the cramp in its stomach! I'd had enough of being buried alive! and I'd had enough of Henry, too! More than enough! I couldn't go on! (*She pauses.*) The rows and the fights were wearing me down! (*Another pause.*) And I wasn't getting any younger, and I wanted a bit of fun before I kicked the bucket.... So I told him. About Len. We weren't rowing or anything. I told him quite quietly one morning. (*Another pause.*) You see, I happened to know Len was in America, and doing very nicely, thanks, with a comfy little apartment of his own, and a photo of me on the piano.... So it seemed the best way to make everybody happy was for me to be there, too.

ALEC (*dryly*). It seemed so to little Meakin, too, I dare say.

MRS DUBINSKI. He looked ten years younger when he skipped off to the shipping office to book my passage, and we were quite pally, bless you, when the time came to say good-bye. Oh, I don't bear little Henry any grudge!

MRS BUTTERWORTH (*heavily sarcastic*). We must tell him that next time we see him. It'll be a load off his mind, I'm sure!

MRS DUBINSKI (*with sudden alarm*). No! No, whatever you do, you'll not tell him I'm in England! You'll not tell anyone! I'm dead and forgotten—in America—and if anyone gets to know different, the game's up, and I'm in for bigamy! No, no, let sleeping dogs lie, *please*, and no harm done!

ALEC (*before* MRS BUTTERWORTH *can speak; brusquely*). Why didn't you stop in America?

MRS DUBINSKI. Lennie had a bit of business here—we only landed last week, and we sail back the day after tomorrow—and I didn't want to be left over there, all by myself.... We're staying in a little hotel off the Gloucester Road, and I haven't stirred out of our room, not once, till this morning.... I thought p'raps I'd risk slipping out for an hour. As there was a fog on, no one'd notice me.

MRS BUTTERWORTH. That'll be why you dressed yourself so quiet, I suppose.

MRS DUBINSKI (*a quick change of tone; pleadingly*). Listen, dear, you'll not split on me, will you? . . . I've made our little place in New York ever so nice. I wish you could see it. The bedroom's all blush-pink, and next year we're going to——

ALEC (*checking her*). That'll be all for now, thank you! (*He jerks his head towards the door.*) Off with you back to America—and see you stop there this time! (*He moves to the fire.*)

MRS DUBINSKI (*staring at him*). You mean . . . ?

ALEC (*bluntly*). Bigamy's not up our street just now. This is your lucky day.

MRS DUBINSKI (*not speaking for a moment; then, scarcely audible*). . . . Thank you. (*She stares for a further second or two; then, suddenly, she starts to hurry towards the door. She pauses half-way. She recovers her self-possession.*) Well, good-bye, Mrs Butterworth. I don't suppose you'll see me again.

(GEORGE *moves up to the door.*)

MRS BUTTERWORTH (*dryly*). No, nor my little enamelled saucepan, neether. Good day to you.

(MRS DUBINSKI *moves up to the door.*)

GEORGE (*meeting her by the door*). Just a minute, please. (*He shifts the mat with his foot and indicates the stain on the floor.*) D'you happen to know anything about that?

MRS DUBINSKI (*stooping a little to peer at the stain, then straightening herself*). Beer, glorious beer, young man! (*Pointing to the top framework of the doorway.*) And that's the *dent* where the bottle found its billet! I never could throw straight!

GEORGE. Thank you.

MRS DUBINSKI. You're welcome, I'm sure.

(GEORGE *opens the door for her, then steps aside. The stable-lamp, still alight, is on the floor of the passage just to* R. *of the cellar door.*)

MRS DUBINSKI (*pausing very briefly in the doorway, assuming a broad Yankee twang*). Wa'al, folks, I sure am glad to have met you! Yeah! (*With a grin and a nod.*) That's me from now on! (*She pulls down her veil.*) Bye-bye!

(*She goes out. The front door slams. There is a very brief pause. Then:*)

MRS BUTTERWORTH (*loudly, towards the doorway*). And a good riddance, too, you rubbish, you! (*Dropping her voice to normal.*) Blush-pink bedroom, indeed! Eeh, I could've said summat, but I didn't . . . ! If I'd been little Meakin, I'd have throttled her ten times over, the trollop!

GEORGE (*coming down* R.C.; *very significantly*). But the point is, he didn't.

ALEC. Not even once. So whoever it is down there, it isn't Cora Meakin, as you call her!

MRS FEARN (*with a little exclamation*). D'you know, just for a minute, I'd forgotten . . . ! George—Francie—you must come with me to Notting Hill at once! We'll get a cab—immediately. . . .

ALEC (*to* GEORGE). Not you! The police'll want to see you. In fact, you'd best come along with me to the station now, and be there when I report.

MRS BUTTERWORTH. Station? You'll find a bobbie soon enough on the Earl's Court Road.

ALEC. We're going to headquarters with this. It isn't a skivvy made off with the spoons, or a kid chucked a brick through a window: it's *murder!*

MRS FEARN. *Oh!* George, close that door, please, I can't bear to see out there!

(GEORGE *moves up towards the door.*)

ALEC (*moving quickly up stage and checking* GEORGE *as he is about to close the door*). Just a minute. I've summat to see to out there first, and I'll thank you for a two-three bits o' sticky paper.

GEORGE. Sticky paper?

FRANCIE (*rising and going to the sideboard*). Would gummed luggage labels do?

ALEC. Aye, they'll do champion.

(GEORGE *moves down to the fireplace.* FRANCIE *opens a drawer and takes from it a packet of gummed labels.*)

MRS FEARN (*agitatedly*). What does he want them for? What's he going to do now? (*To* ALEC.) You're not going down into that awful place again, I should hope!

ALEC (*taking the labels from* FRANCIE). Ta.

(*He goes out into the passage, closing the door behind him.*)

MRS FEARN. George, what's he going to do?

(FRANCIE *moves down* L. *to* MRS FEARN.)

GEORGE. How should I know?

FRANCIE. Try not to be too upset, Mother. It can't do any good now, you know.

MRS FEARN. I can't think why you're so calm about it all at once, Francie. You were upset enough yourself, just now. You were terrified!

FRANCIE. Only because we didn't know what. . . . Now that we do know, I'm not afraid any more.

MRS BUTTERWORTH (*with sudden inspiration; to* MRS FEARN). I'll tell you what: you come next door with me, and I'll make you a nice strong cup o' tea—real mahogany colour—and a drop o' summat in it! (*She takes her scarf from the easy chair and flings it loosely round her neck as she starts to go to the door.*) I'll just slip along and put a match to sitting-room fire.—Eeh, and I've just remembered, I left some cow-heel stewing! Oh, my Lord. (*She hurries to the door and reaches it at the same moment as* ALEC *opens it from the outside.*) Out of my way, lad! (*To* MRS FEARN.) Front door'll be off chain, so walk straight in!

E

(*She bustles off. The front door slams.* ALEC *comes into the room, leaving the door open. He has pasted several of the strips of paper round the edges of the cellar door, sealing it.*)

GEORGE. What . . . ?

ALEC (*crossing to the fireplace; importantly*). Just a matter of official procedure. (*He puts the rest of the labels on the mantelshelf.*)

FRANCIE. What about the other door that leads into the yard?

ALEC. Eh? (*Hesitating—frowning.*) Oh, let it go! There isn't time! (*He takes the ear-ring from the mantelshelf.*) And see, let nobody meddle with this here! This'll be a very important exhibit at the trial!

GEORGE. Trial? Aren't we being a bit previous?

ALEC. Don't worry. There'll be a trial all right. I can feel it in my bones! (*He replaces the ear-ring on the mantelshelf, so that it is rather more forward and prominent than before.*)

MRS FEARN (*faintly*). Oh!——

GEORGE (*to* MRS FEARN). What's the matter now?

MRS FEARN (*weakly*). Bones. . . .

FRANCIE (*going to her*). Mother—please—do go along now, and have that cup of tea! It'll revive you.

MRS FEARN. Yes—yes, I must—I feel, if I stay in this place another minute, I shall be *ill*! (*Plaintively.*) George, why did your uncle have to choose this one house out of the whole of London? *The whole of London? I ask* you!

FRANCIE (*quickly*). Never mind about that now! (*Comfortingly.*) There'll be a lovely cup of tea for you next door, and I'll follow you there, presently. (*She leads* MRS FEARN *below the table and up* C.) Now, come along, dear, do!

MRS FEARN (*allowing herself to be led*). You're being so brave about it all now, Francie, aren't you? So calm. It's from my side of the family, you know. Your father's people were a dreadfully highly-strung lot. Two of his sisters used to cry every time they heard church bells, and his mother always kept three nightlights burning. . . . (*They are out in the passage now. Finding herself facing the cellar door, she starts back with a little scream.*) Oh! !——

(*Tightening her grip on her mother's arm,* FRANCIE *hurries* MRS FEARN *off. The front door is heard to close.*)

ALEC (*moving below the table*). And you, look sharp and get your things on and we'll make tracks for the police station. We've wasted too much time, as it is, mucking about!

(FRANCIE *enters and comes to* L. *of* GEORGE.)

(*To* FRANCIE.) Aye, and you'll wait here, till we're back, see?

GEORGE (*instantly*). What? D'you think I'm going to leave my wife in this house alone? What d'you take me for? (*To*

FRANCIE.) I won't hear of it, Francie! (*To* ALEC.) You'll have to go by yourself!

ALEC. I'd as lief you come with me, all the same. (*To* FRANCIE.) Auntie and your ma'll have to come back and stop with you, that's all. I'll fetch 'em! (*He moves quickly up to the door. To* GEORGE.) You be getting your things on!

(*As* ALEC *reaches the doorway, there is a sharp rap on the french window. He halts. A split second of silence. The three look quickly towards the curtained window.*)

FRANCIE. Madam! She was coming in to show me her new dress! What shall I do?

ALEC (*thinking quickly*). Let her in! She's just in time! *She'll* do for company for you!

GEORGE. But—supposing she only stays a minute——

ALEC. A minute, and come to talk about dress? Don't talk soft! (*To* FRANCIE.) Let her in!

(FRANCIE *crosses above the table.*)

Here, wait!

(FRANCIE *pauses.*)

You'll say naught about aught, mind! Talk about finery and fal-lals as much as you like—but keep right off murder, see?

GEORGE. But they'll know soon enough, surely.

ALEC. "Soon enough" 'll be after the police have taken charge —not before! (*To* FRANCIE.) So keep your mouth shut! *And* this door, too! Don't let anyone see out here!

(*There is another rap on the window.*)

FRANCIE (*quietly*). All right. I understand.

ALEC (*to* GEORGE). I'll slip into Auntie's for my things, and meet you outside! I shan't be a sec., so look sharp! (*To* FRANCIE.) Go on! Let her in!

(*He hurries off. The front door slams.* FRANCIE *starts again for the window. Before she quite reaches it,* GEORGE *hurries to her, takes her quickly in his arms, and kisses her.*)

GEORGE. Darling, are you sure you'll be all right?

FRANCIE (*with a quick nod*). I've said I'm not afraid any more, haven't I? Darling. . . .

(*Another snatched kiss, then* GEORGE *releases her, goes up stage and out into the passage, closing the door behind him.* FRANCIE *has gone to the window. She does not draw the curtains, but thrusts her hand through them and undoes the catch, then holds them aside as* MADAM *enters. . . .* MADAM's *appearance is both striking and dramatic, her dress being almost entirely concealed by a voluminous, swansdown-edged cloak of brilliant scarlet, which latter is seen to be lined with white quilted satin.*

A white lace scarf is draped over her head and round her throat, and she is carrying a white sequin-starred fan. As she enters, she is holding up her skirt, which she drops as soon as she is in the room.)

MADAM (*as she enters; with a sort of breathless excitement*). My dear, tell me you don't think this quite mad of me! But the dress arrived just now, and I simply *had* to try it on! (*She comes below the table.*) Have I splashed my pretty shoes? No! Aren't they darling little shoes? See the buckles!

FRANCIE. They're lovely. (*She comes down* L.)

(During the following scene, FRANCIE is straining every nerve to appear quite normal and natural.)

MADAM. I *do* like shoes and gloves to be *good*, don't you? They make all the difference to one's toilette! Even when we'd only a little money, Neville and I, I'd always have the *best* shoes and gloves! Don't you think this cloak's rather sumptuous? I do! (*Turning round to display it.*) Look!

FRANCIE (*quite genuinely captivated for the moment*). It's very, very handsome! It's beautiful!

MADAM. I'm so glad you—Ah!

(She breaks off, as the door opens a little way to admit GEORGE's head and shoulders. He is wearing an overcoat.)

GEORGE. I'm going now, darling. You're sure you'll be all right? (*To* MADAM.) Good afternoon.

FRANCIE. Quite all right, George.

MADAM. You're going out?

GEORGE. I shall be back very soon. Will you do me a favour, and keep Francie company while I'm away?

MADAM. Of course I will! But you must tell me first if you like my cloak!

GEORGE. It's a truly magnificent cloak, Madam . . . and you look magnificent in it.

MADAM (*gaily—with a little curtsy*). Thank you, sir!

GEORGE (*to* FRANCIE). Au revoir, then, darling.

(A swift look of understanding flashes between them, then he goes, closing the door quietly behind him. The front door is also heard to close.)

MADAM. What an utterly charming man he is, dear! So very . . . (*She breaks off, apparently noticing for the first time.*) But why—why the drawn curtains and the lights?

FRANCIE. It was so dark—the fog.

MADAM. But the fog's lifted now.

FRANCIE (*moving to the window*). Oh——

MADAM (*quickly*). No, no, leave it as it is! The dress will look better by gas-light! (*She sweeps towards down* R.)

(FRANCIE moves a little down stage L. *of the table.)*

Stay where you are! (*With a dramatic movement, she flings wide her cloak, slips it from her shoulders, and tosses it on to the armchair down* R.) There!

(*The gown is a quite breath-taking affair of white satin very décolleté, and elaborately trimmed with frothing cascades of lace and glittering sequins. It is, in fact, a quite startlingly handsome dress of the period. With it* MADAM *is wearing long white gloves.*)

FRANCIE (*captivated again*). Yes! Oh, yes . . . ! Oh, it *is* lovely, *isn't* it?

MADAM. Well, frankly, *I* think it is! I mean it's quite clear that I haven't run it up myself, isn't it? It *looks* expensive!

FRANCIE. It's *beautiful*!

MADAM. One can never go wrong with satin, can one? Especially for the concert platform. (*Unwinding the scarf.*) I put on my gloves, too: I wanted you to see the whole effect.

FRANCIE. You look . . . very, very wonderful, Madam.

MADAM (*pleased*). Really? How nice of you to say so. (*She tosses the scarf on to the armchair. In her hair is a star of brilliants.*) And, of course, one's appearance on a platform does help. I'm sure I sing all the better, if I know that I'm *looking* well! . . . The *Standard's* got a little bit about last night's concert, and of course it mentions me. Not much, but *quite* nice. Neville shall show it to you when he comes. He said he'd follow me in a few minutes. Oh, and the fan! (*Flicking it open.*) Do tell me you like it!

FRANCIE. It's very pretty indeed.

MADAM. I was torn between this and a feather one! The little gold stars decided me! (*Moving it to catch the light.*) Look how they glitter!

FRANCIE. . . . Yes. (*She sits rather abruptly* R. *of the table.*)

(MADAM *looks at her, snaps her fan to, and moves a little nearer to her.*)

MADAM. Is it the light, or are you really looking just a wee bit pale? Aren't you feeling well?

FRANCIE (*rallying herself and forcing a little smile*). Quite well. . . . A little headache, perhaps.

MADAM. You poor dear! I had a tiny migraine myself this morning.

(*There is a tap on the french window.*)

Hark! That will be Neville!—No, don't get up—I'll——

(*With a rustle and swish of satin, she half-runs towards the window, crossing above the table. Before she quite reaches it, the curtains are parted, and the* PROFESSOR *enters. He takes one step into the room, then halts.*)

THE PROFESSOR. What are you doing, Mildred?

(FRANCIE *rises.*)

MADAM. Hurrying to open the window for you, dear.

THE PROFESSOR. Thank you, my love, but it happened to be off the catch. (*He comes below the table. To* FRANCIE; *more genially.*) And how is our little bride this afternoon? My wife insisted on exhibiting herself to you in her new frills and fur-belows! She hasn't wearied you, I hope.

MADAM (*before* FRANCIE *can reply; coming down* L.). Our poor little bride has a headache, Neville.

THE PROFESSOR. Ah! Silks and satins and headaches! Could anything be more deliciously feminine? (*He takes a step towards* FRANCIE; *with a change of manner.*) Seriously, though, I'm sorry.

FRANCIE. It's nothing, really.

THE PROFESSOR (*moving up to* FRANCIE *and looking at her more closely*). M'm . . . a strained look about the eyes. . . . The excitement of a new life in a new house, no doubt. It will pass.

MADAM. But it's a darling house, and you *do* like it, don't you, dear? (*She flicks her fan open, flitting it to and fro, to catch the light.*)

FRANCIE. We . . . hardly know, yet.

THE PROFESSOR. Oh, you will, you will! (*He strolls down* R.) Just give yourselves time to get properly settled. It's the kind of house that very soon gets a hold on you, from attic to . . . *wine*-cellar. *Wine*-cellar! (*A little, dry chuckle.*) A harmless little conceit of mine, eh?

MADAM (*who has moved slowly up* L.). Tell me, do, how does it look from the back? (*She moves above the table to up* C.)

FRANCIE. Very well indeed. (*She moves towards* MADAM.)

MADAM (*posing; her back to the audience*). It hangs well, you think?

THE PROFESSOR (*picking up the cloak from the armchair and studying it*). It hangs as neatly and sweetly, my love, as a knave from the tree at Tyburn.

MADAM (*turning quickly—snapping her fan to*). Neville! *What* a disgusting thing to say! Really! And please put that down at once! You'll crush it!

(*In attempting to replace the cloak, the* PROFESSOR *misses the chair, and the cloak falls to the floor.*)

There! Look what you've done!

(*She starts to the rescue.* FRANCIE, *with a little* "Oh!" *does the same. Before either of them arrive, the* PROFESSOR *has stooped and picked up the cloak.*)

THE PROFESSOR (*handing the cloak to* MADAM). The hysterical fuss you women make about your clothes!

(*The three are now just below the fireplace. Having handed the cloak to* MADAM, *the* PROFESSOR *steps back a pace.* FRANCIE *and* MADAM *are now facing one another, with a space of about two yards between them.* . . . *And on the corsage of* MADAM's *gown is a little glittering object that has caught and held* FRANCIE's *eye. Her whole body suddenly rigid, she stares and stares.*)

MADAM (*as she takes the cloak*). There's nothing hysterical in handling pretty things with care! You might have ruined it! (*Becoming aware of* FRANCIE's *look.*) What's the matter, dear? Is anything . . . (*She looks down at the front of her dress.*)

FRANCIE (*in a small, dry voice*). Your—brooch, Madam.

MADAM (*her hand flying to it—fingering it*). Is it undone?

FRANCIE (*shaking her head—still staring at it*). No. . . . (*With an effort to speak quite calmly.*) I was just thinking . . . it's a very lovely brooch . . . a little crescent moon and star. . . .

MADAM. It hasn't always been a brooch. It was an ear-ring, once: one of a pair belonging to a very dear friend of ours, poor Miss Barrett, who died at Tunbridge Wells.

THE PROFESSOR (*moving to the fireplace; lightly*). Actually, Miss Barrett had an execrable taste in jewellery. That particular ornament was one of her least objectionable trinkets.

MADAM. The others were frightful. I've kept them, of course. They were so much a part of *her*, I could never bring myself to sell them. In all my thoughts of her, she's wearing them . . . bangles and brooches and chains, and always that sad, bewildered look on her face.

THE PROFESSOR (*resting one hand on the mantelshelf*). Miss Barrett *looked* bewildered because she *was* bewildered. Her mental machinery had quite run down. In a very little while she'd have . . . (*His eyes have suddenly lighted on some object on the mantelshelf— he stops abruptly.*)

FRANCIE. But . . . the other ear-ring?

THE PROFESSOR (*his eyes still fixed on that tiny object; slowly*). She —must have lost it—we think.

MADAM. So I had this one made into a brooch. (*Looking at* FRANCIE—*smiling.*) How nice of you to admire it. (*The smile vanishing.*) My dear, your headache! Quite suddenly, you look all white and drawn!

FRANCIE (*turning away—one hand to her face—striving to control herself.*) A little. . . . (*She moves* L.)

MADAM (*solicitously*). You poor soul! Sit down and lean back, do, and let me stroke your forehead. I often used to for Miss Barrett.

FRANCIE (*drawing back*). No—no—— (*With rather more control.*) I'm all right, it's nothing.

(*The* PROFESSOR *has turned a little away from the fireplace. There is an air of tension about him, but his expression, save that the line of his mouth has hardened, is unchanged, and gives nothing away.*)

THE PROFESSOR (*almost before* FRANCIE *has finished speaking— quietly, but with an underlying note of command—not looking directly at her*). Mildred, I have a sudden presentiment of danger. You will go back into the house at once, please.

MADAM. Danger?

THE PROFESSOR (*not looking at either of them*). We—er—left a large fire in the sitting-room grate. If a live coal were to fly out, the whole place could be ablaze.

MADAM. Oh, don't be silly, Neville!

THE PROFESSOR (*the note of command very evident now*). Silly I may be, but I prefer not to take risks! Put on your cloak, Mildred, and don't argue! (*He takes her scarf from the chair.*) Your scarf! (*He holds it out to her at arm's length.*)

MADAM. But—I promised I'd keep our little bride company.

THE PROFESSOR. I propose to give myself that pleasure. (*Still holding out the scarf.*) Make haste, if you please.

MADAM. But, good heaven . . . ! (*Breaking off and catching her breath.*) Neville—is there anything wrong?

THE PROFESSOR (*his voice sharp-edged*). Will you kindly stop asking questions, and do as I say! (*With more control.*) You've done no practice today. Go and sing, my love. Your singing last evening was not entirely flawless.

MADAM (*about to protest—then giving in and starting to wrap her cloak round her; to* FRANCIE, *half-humorously*). You see what a poor down-trodden wretch I am! (*To the* PROFESSOR.) You and your presentiments! It's a pity I didn't have one before I married you! (*She snatches the scarf from him with mock impatience; to* FRANCIE.) He's crazed on the subject of fire, and I have to humour him.

(*The* PROFESSOR *crosses above the table to the window.*)

(*She flings the scarf over her head.*) I tell him the devil will have a lovely time, later, tormenting him with little green and red flames!

(*The* PROFESSOR *thrusts his hand through the curtains and opens the window.*)

THE PROFESSOR (*very straight and direct*). Mildred!

MADAM (*to* FRANCIE). I'm so sorry to run away like this, and I do hope your poor head will soon be better. (*She kisses her.*)

(*Involuntarily,* FRANCIE *flinches and draws back.*)

Oh, my dear, I'm sorry. Some people don't like to be kissed, I know. Forgive me.

THE PROFESSOR (*very insistently and with a little tap of his foot on the floor*). Mildred!

MADAM (*quickly; in a whisper*). Good-bye.

FRANCIE (*with an effort*). Good-bye.

(MADAM *hastens to the window.*)

MADAM (*giving the* PROFESSOR *a little tap with her fan as she passes him*). Oh, you ruthless, domineering man, you!

(*The* Professor *is holding the curtains a little aside.* Madam *passes through, and is gone.* Francie *crosses down* R. *of the table. Thrusting his arm through the curtains, the* Professor *pulls the window to: one hears the click of the catch, and* Francie *and the* Professor *are alone, he by the window, she* R. *a little below the table, facing him across the room. There is silence, fairly long and very tense. His eyes are fixed unswervingly upon her. She, filled with an increasing but as yet nameless fear, forces herself to return his look. Then, slowly, his gaze travels from her to the mantelshelf, to the little glittering object lying there. Slowly, too, her own look follows his, her head turns slightly. They are both looking at the mantelshelf. The next moment they are looking at one another again across the room . . . and her fear is no longer nameless.*)

The Professor (*his voice dead level*). Well?

(Francie *gives a little convulsive jerk at the sound of his voice.*)

(*Still in that dead-level tone.*) Where was it? Where did you find it?

(Francie's *mouth works—she tries to speak—but no sound comes.*)

Where?

Francie (*at last—forcing out the words*). I—don't know.

The Professor (*not speaking for a moment—his eyes narrowing, but never shifting from her; then, his voice still dead level*). But you do know —what I'm speaking of, don't you? You know very well, I think!

Francie (*she, too, not speaking for a moment; then, quite suddenly steeling herself to a sort of reckless courage—an odd, sharp edge to her voice*). Yes! Yes, I do! The other ear-ring—that was lost! (*Her voice snaps off.*)

The Professor (*not raising his voice*). And is now lying there, on your mantelshelf—so strangely and miraculously restored.

Francie (*as before—her whole body stiff as a rod—the sharp edge to her voice more pronounced*). Miss Barrett's ear-ring. (*Still sharper— louder.*) Miss Barrett! Who lived in your house—and who did not die at Tunbridge Wells!

(*A split second of silence. The* Professor *makes no movement.*)

You'll have to be quick—won't you—if you're going to kill me— as you killed her?

(*Another split second of silence.*)

There won't be time to hide me away, though—like you hid her! There won't be time, will there?

(*Silence. The* Professor *is still looking at her through those narrowed lids. Then, never taking his eyes off her, he puts his right hand slowly into his jacket pocket, and draws from it a small revolver.* Francie *gives a little choking gasp. One hand flies to her mouth.*)

(*Involuntarily; quite loudly, but muffled by her hand.*) Oh, no!

THE PROFESSOR. Stay exactly where you are! Don't move! (*He goes quickly to the door, and flings it open. The white paper seals on the cellar door stare him in the face. One glance, then he turns swiftly to face back into the room. He is breathing a shade more quickly than normal.*) I see . . . ! So—the game is up—quite—up, eh?

FRANCIE (*taking her hand from her mouth and jerking the words out*). Hadn't you better go now? My husband will be back—any minute!

THE PROFESSOR. Accompanied by half the police force of Kensington, no doubt! (*He shrugs, and with the shrug his manner seems to change completely. It is no longer quite so menacing; instead, it suggests rather, a kind of grim, sardonic acceptance. He comes down stage a few steps.*) All the same, I think I'll risk that minute. (*He moves above the table.*) And I think I'd like you to sit down.

(FRANCIE *hesitates, then, as though compelled, she makes a movement as though to sit down* R.)

No, no—not over there! (*Pointing to the chair* R. *of the table.*) Here!

(FRANCIE *hesitates, then goes to the chair and sits. A further second, then the* PROFESSOR *too sits, above the table. He places the revolver on the table, in front and slightly to* L. *of him.* FRANCIE *stares at it with horrified fascination.*)

(*Noting her look.*) I carry it about with me always. A minor eccentricity, perhaps. . . . Quite tiny, but quite deadly.

FRANCIE (*in spite of herself*). You—killed her with that?

THE PROFESSOR. You—really want all the details?

FRANCIE (*shrinking back in her chair*). No, no——

(*A barely perceptible pause. Then:*)

THE PROFESSOR (*quietly*). You're—very frightened, aren't you?

FRANCIE (*after a moment; scarcely audible*). Yes—very.

THE PROFESSOR (*with a sort of quiet candour*). So was I, just now, when I saw that jewel winking at me from your mantelshelf. The whole world turned to ice in a single second, and I was quite indescribably afraid. But, oddly enough, I'm not any more. I'm quite calm now. That's funny, isn't it?

FRANCIE (*still scarcely audible*). I—don't know.

THE PROFESSOR (*after a moment; almost casually*). You needn't waste too much womanly sympathy on *her*, by the way . . . Miss Barrett; a witless, silly creature, of unpleasing habits. With nothing to look forward to but the madhouse—and that very soon. Death was a mercy, really—especially when it came so swiftly and unknowingly.

(FRANCIE *forces herself to look at him.*)

I shot her from behind. She was sitting at a little table, playing

what she ludicrously imagined was a game of Patience. It was all
over in a second. She didn't move, she just sat there—quite still,
of course. (*He pauses.*)

(FRANCIE's *gaze shifts to the revolver.*)

(*He touches it lightly.*) The handle's real mother-of-pearl, by the
way.

FRANCIE (*as though the exclamation is wrung from her*). Oh!

THE PROFESSOR (*raising his eyebrows slightly*). Yes?

FRANCIE. Oh! *How* can you talk like this? How can you sit
there and—and—— (*Her voice breaks off in a little sob.*)

THE PROFESSOR (*calmly, smoothly*). My dear young lady, think:
the span of my life has quite suddenly contracted to the size of a
very little bridge over a very little stream. I prefer to wend my
brief way over it with as little fuss and melodrama as possible,
if you don't mind.

FRANCIE. But—you murdered her! Coldly and deliberately, you
murdered her!

THE PROFESSOR (*with one slow nod of assent*). Quite coldly and
quite deliberately, I'm glad to say! If I'd killed in a moment of
brutal, animal passion, I should never have forgiven myself. My
—er—elimination of Miss Barrett was the result of reason and
clear thinking. There she was, with her money, and not a wish
in the world, save to eat and sleep and fumble with a dirty pack
of cards: and there were we, I tutoring a few backward boys for
a pittance, Mildred airing a third-rate voice at third-rate concerts, to scrape in a few extra guineas . . . ! The gnawing misery
of it . . . ! Can you even begin to understand?

FRANCIE. . . . No!

THE PROFESSOR (*with a degree of quiet scorn*). No, of course you
can't. You belong to the class that'll make itself dizzy turning
the other cheek to Fate!

(*A pause. He rises, and starts to move down L. FRANCIE's eyes are again
upon the revolver. During the following speech, for the first second or two,
she seems not to realize the significance of its lying there, unguarded.
Then the situation flashes upon her. She glances quickly towards him. His
back is turned to her. Very slowly, her hand starts to slide across the
table to the revolver.*)

Mildred, of course, still sings at concerts, but for vanity now,
not money. She sees herself as a great *diva*. She wears magnificent gowns these days, and her fancy's vivid enough to turn a
dreary suburban assembly-room into a great and glittering con-
cert-hall. Childish, of course, but it does no harm. Admiration
and applause are oysters and champagne to Mildred. Just now,
displaying her jewels and her new dress, she was in Paradise.
(*He turns abruptly and sees her hand.*)

(*Obeying some reflex impulse rather than reason,* FRANCIE *withdraws her hand immediately. The* PROFESSOR *betrays no reaction, but moves quite leisurely up* L. *of the table, picks up the revolver, and slips it into his jacket pocket.*)

(*He continues in the same tone.*) There's no denying, of course, she has good taste. Flamboyant at times, perhaps, but good. (*A short pause. He comes down stage, crosses below the table and moves up* c.) One thing, believe me, I do apologize for: the dismal use to which we put your cellar. How *did* you come to—er—investigate, by the way?

FRANCIE (*at the end of endurance*). Oh, *please*. . . .

THE PROFESSOR (*turning to her; quickly*). Quite! Quite! An indelicate question—forgive me! (*He looks towards the mantelshelf.*) The ear-ring, though, I really would like to know—just how—where . . .

FRANCIE. I can't——

THE PROFESSOR (*as before*). No, no—and it can't matter now, can it? The hand of Justice? God? Or just plain bad luck?

(FRANCIE *rises suddenly.*)

Where are you going?

FRANCIE (*urgently*). Let me go now—*please*—out into the street —anywhere—I can't stay here——

THE PROFESSOR. I'm sorry—but no. (*He looks at her with just a faint trace of smile.*) You're not appreciating it now, of course— but this, you know, is one of the really great moments of your life. Something you'll remember to your dying day. "My *tête-à-tête* with a murderer." Just think how your grand-children will revel in it.

FRANCIE (*desperately*). I've told you—my husband . . .

THE PROFESSOR. Will be back at any moment—and *not* alone! Thank you for reminding me. My tongue is apt to run away with me when I find a good listener. But I mustn't overstay my welcome. No. (*Again with a faint trace of a smile.*) To know just when to leave . . . that is the thing! (*He crosses her to go above the table to the window, stops, pauses, then slowly turns and looks at her. Rather slowly; thoughtfully.*) It's just occurred to me: Miss Barrett never wore those ear-rings. . . . No one knew she possessed them. . . . And Mildred had never worn that damnable brooch before today. . . . So, you see, you're the only living soul at this moment who really *knows*. . . . Let us suppose, now, that you suddenly ceased to be a living soul . . . would I stand a chance? (*He pauses, frowning thoughtfully. His hand strays towards his jacket pocket. Still thinking.*) D'you know, I rather fancy . . . *not!* (*A shorter pause; then with a decisive shake of his head.*) No!

(*He goes to the window and draws the curtains apart. The fog has now quite lifted, and the frosted branches of the plane tree are glittering in the*

*red light of the setting sun. He thrusts open the french window. The
sound of a piano can be faintly heard.*)

Look at that! Snow and ice . . . and the sun going down blood-
red. (*A very short pause.*) I'd have liked to get a little drunk, I think,
on very old brandy, but I'm afraid there isn't time.

(*There is a loud rap at the front door.*)

FRANCIE (*the back of her hand to her mouth; looking wildly up stage;
then at him*). They're here! Now! What're you going to do? (*She
makes a quick move towards the door.*)

THE PROFESSOR (*hearing her movement; not turning; sharply*). Not
yet! Stay where you are till I've gone, then let them in!

(FRANCIE *pauses, half-way to the door. The* PROFESSOR *stands for a
moment, framed in the window opening, very stiff and erect, his head held
high. There is a louder, more insistent knocking.*)

FRANCIE. *Oh!*

THE PROFESSOR (*not moving*). What does it say in that book that
everybody quotes? . . . "The world passeth away, and the lust
thereof."

(*A second's pause. The piano ceases.*)

Now!

(*He thrusts one hand into his jacket pocket. Then, with head still high,
he steps out quickly from the window, and is gone.* FRANCIE *stands for
a moment, unable to move. Then, suddenly, she dashes out of the room,
into the passage, and off. The next instant* GEORGE's *voice is heard.*)

GEORGE (*off*). Francie—are you all right? Have I been a long
time?

(*He hurries in, struggling out of his coat.* FRANCIE *follows him.*)

(*Breathlessly; looking hastily round the room.*) Where's Madam? Has
she . . . ? Darling, you *haven't* been alone all this time! And why's
that window open? (*He tosses his coat on to the chair* R. *of the table,
looks at* FRANCIE *quickly and goes to her.*) What's the matter? Francie,
what's happened?

FRANCIE (*fighting for control*). Where are they—the police?

GEORGE. They're on their way. They'll be here in a minute! I
ran on ahead! (*He breaks off, grasps her shoulders and looks at her
anxiously.*) Darling, don't look like that—please! There's nothing
more to worry about! It's all over now! It's all over, Francie!

FRANCIE (*not listening; her ears straining to catch some sound from
outside*). Hush!

(*The piano has started again; a few introductory bars to "The Last Rose
of Summer". And now,* MADAM *commences to sing.*)

GEORGE. What's the matter?

(FRANCIE *suddenly thrusts him from her, turns swiftly, and half-runs to the window. There she halts abruptly, and stands, her back to the room, very tense and upright.)*

(*He stares at her; then hurries across to her.*) Francie—what is it? What's happening out there?

FRANCIE (*without changing her attitude*). Be very quiet, George— and listen!

         (GEORGE *halts immediately behind her.*)

   GEORGE. Well? I can hear Madam singing—that's all.

   FRANCIE (*suddenly turning to face him; forcing herself to speak quite calmly and enunciating each word very clearly*). George, you're not to think I'm being hysterical or silly! You've got to believe what I tell you! Those two in the next house—the Professor and Madam —they killed Miss Barrett—he shot her in the back—(*her self-control breaking for a moment*) in the back, George!

   GEORGE (*staring at her; not immediately grasping her words*). What on earth are you talking about.

   FRANCIE (*silencing him with a gesture*). Hush . . . ! Is she—is she still singing?

   GEORGE (*impatiently*). Can't you hear her? Look here, Francie, what's all this about Miss Barrett?

   FRANCIE. Ssh!

(*There is a split second's pause. Then three things happen almost simultaneously; the sharp crack of a shot, the sudden snapping-off of* MADAM'S *voice in mid-note, and a crashing discord on the piano.*)

   GEORGE (*sharply*). What's that? A shot? (*He makes a movement as though to pass* FRANCIE.)

   FRANCIE (*barring the way*). No, no, wait! Let him do it this way! It's better, George, it's better like this—please! Please!

   GEORGE. You're talking in riddles, and I want to know what's going on out there! Let me pass, Francie!

(*He is about to push past her, when he is checked by the sound of another shot. Instinctively they clutch at one another, and stand immovable, their heads turned to look out in the direction of the shot.*)

(*Quietly.*) Francie. . . .

         (FRANCIE *turns slowly towards him.*)

   FRANCIE (*haltingly; still quietly*). Can't you picture them . . . ? He's stretched out on the floor—staring up at the ceiling. . . . She's on her knees by the piano—with her head on the stool. . . . They look awful, George . . . like two big dolls. . . . *Awful!*

   GEORGE. Francie, dearest . . . ! Don't . . . ! Please, don't!

There is a thunderous knocking at the front door. They hold each other more tightly, their heads turned in the direction of this new sound, as—

       the CURTAIN *slowly falls.*

FURNITURE AND PROPERTY PLOT

GROUND PLAN

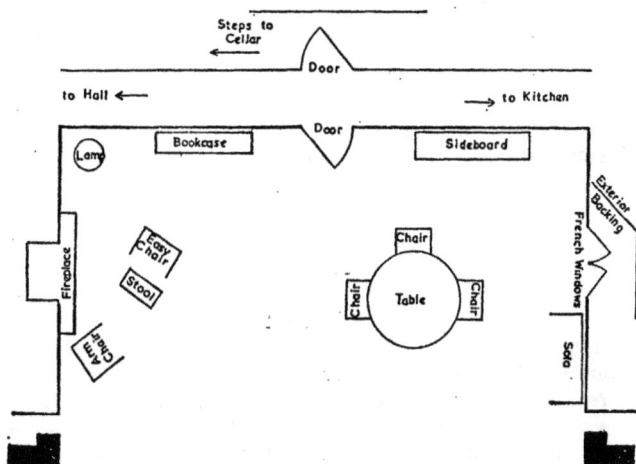

ACT I

On stage:

Sofa. *On it:* 2 cushions.
Round table. *On it:* tablecloth.
3 Upright chairs.
Armchair.
Easy chair.
Footstool.
Sideboard. *On it:* tantalus, cake-dish, egg-cup stand, reading
          lamp, 2 vases, other items as required to dress.
       In cupboard: bottle of wine, tray, 6 glasses, work-
          basket, sock.
Bookcase. *On it:* marble bust.
Standard lamp.
On mantelpiece: glass-cased clock, 2 bronze figures, 2 vases,
   candle-stick.
In fireplace: fire-irons, hearth-brush.

At window: pelmet, heavy curtains to draw.
Umbrella-stand (wrapped).
Carpet, doormat.
Pictures.

Off stage R.:
　Plate of oat-cakes (MRS BUTTERWORTH).
　Newspaper (GEORGE).
　Lantern (ALEC).

Off stage L.:
　Bellows (MRS FEARN).

Personal:
　PROFESSOR: handkerchief.
　GEORGE: matches.

ACT II

SCENE 1

On stage:
　Strike: all glasses, newspaper.
　Replace: On table: white tablecloth, 4 plates, 2 cups and saucers,
　　2 knives, teapot, milk-jug, sugar basin, toast-rack, butter-
　　dish, egg-cup with empty shell, egg-cup with unbroken shell
　　(FRANCIE), 2 egg-spoons, slop basin, cruet.

Off stage R.:
　Newspaper (GEORGE).
　Lantern (ALEC).

Off stage L.:
　3 white roses (MADAM).
　Tray (FRANCIE).

Personal:
　FRANCIE: handkerchief.
　GEORGE: pocket watch.

SCENE 2

On stage:
　Move: MRS FEARN's chair to face audience, work-basket and
　　socks to middle of table.
　Set: inkstand, pen, sheet of notepaper on table before FRANCIE.

Off stage R.:
　Lantern (ALEC).

Personal:
　ALEC: ear-ring.

ACT III

On stage:
  Set: On sideboard: glass.
    In sideboard drawer: luggage labels.
    On passage floor, R. *of cellar door:* lantern.
  Check: wine bottle on sideboard; ear-ring on mantelpiece.

Personal:
  MADAM: brooch.
  PROFESSOR: revolver.

EFFECTS PLOT

ACT I

To open. Cellar door closed.
  Sound of MADAM singing scales.

Cue *1.* MRS FEARN *kneels at the fireplace and uses bellows.*
  Cellar door opens.

Cue *2.* MRS FEARN *closes the french windows.*
  Singing fades out.

Cue *3.* MRS FEARN *tucks paper behind sofa cushion.*
  Knock at front door.

Cue *4.* MRS FEARN. ". . . even the house itself!"
  MRS BUTTERWORTH. "No!"
  Cellar door opens.

Cue *5.* MRS BUTTERWORTH. "He's down with me from Burnley
    for a fortnight . . ."
  Fade in sound of approaching cab.

Cue *6.* MRS FEARN. "They've got a key!"
  Cab stops.

Cue *7.* PROFESSOR. "It makes it seem less chill, somehow."
  Knock at front door.

Cue *8.* GEORGE. ". . . was executed at Newgate yesterday morn-
    ing."
  Knock at front door.

Cue *9.* GEORGE *opens the french windows.*
  Sound of MADAM singing "The Last Rose of Summer".

Cue *10.* GEORGE *and* FRANCIE *listen to the singing for a moment.*
  Click of latch.
  Cellar door opens.

F

ACT II

SCENE 1

Cue 11. MADAM. ". . . even an east wind is no excuse for cheap cynicism."
Knock at front door.

Cue 12. FRANCIE. "Oh, George!" (*Somewhat reassured she is about to sit in the easy chair.*)
Hollow thud from cellar.

Cue 13. MRS FEARN. ". . . Be quiet, will you!" (*She moves to L. of FRANCIE.*)
They pause for a second and listen.
Sound of heavy footsteps on cellar steps.

Cue 14. FRANCIE (*hysterically*). "Where are you going? No! Come back! George!"
Loud rat-tat on cellar door.

Cue 15. ALEC. ". . . We'll see what we shall see—eh?"
A very short silence.
The cellar door opens.

Cue 16. GEORGE (*still looking towards the door; quite softly*). "Ssh!"
Sound of pick-axe.

SCENE 2

Cue 17. ALEC. ". . . —and his name's Meakin!"
Loud rap on front door.

ACT III

Cue 18. MRS DUBINSKI. ". . . Bye-bye!" (*She goes.*)
Front door slams.

Cue 19. MRS BUTTERWORTH. ". . . Front door'll be off chain, so walk straight in!" (*She bustles off.*)
Front door slams.

Cue 20. FRANCIE *leads* MRS FEARN *off*.
Front door closes (light slam).

Cue 21. ALEC. ". . . You be getting your things on!"
Rap on window.

Cue 22. ALEC. ". . . Don't let anyone see out here!"
Rap on window.

Cue 23. ALEC *hurries off.*
Front door slams.

Cue 24. GEORGE. "Au revoir, then, darling." (*He goes.*)
Front door closes (light slam).

Cue 25. MADAM. ". . . I had a tiny migraine this morning."
Tap on window.

Cue 26. PROFESSOR *opens the window.*
Fade in piano.

Cue 27. PROFESSOR. ". . . but I'm afraid there isn't time."
Loud rap on front door knocker.

Cue 28. PROFESSOR. ". . . then let them in!" (*He stands framed in the window opening.*)
Loud rap on front door knocker.

Cue 29. PROFESSOR. ". . . The world passeth away, and the lust thereof."
Piano stops.

Cue 30. GEORGE. ". . . It's all over now!"
Piano starts "Last Rose of Summer".

Cue 31. FRANCIE. "Hush!"
MADAM sings.

Cue 32. GEORGE. ". . . what's all this about Miss Barrett?"
FRANCIE. "Ssh!" (*There is a brief pause.*)
1. Shot.
2. MADAM's voice snaps off.
3. Discord on piano.

Cue 33. GEORGE. ". . . Let me pass, Francie!"
Shot.

Cue 34. GEORGE. "Francie, dearest . . . ! Don't . . . ! Please, don't!"
Thunderous knocking at front door.

LIGHTING PLOT

Property fittings required:
  2 Gas brackets (practical).
  Standard lamp—oil (not practical).
  Table lamp—oil (not practical) .
  Stable lantern (practical).

BATTENS *or* FLOODS should be used for the general lighting from above. (*Suitable colours are 3 Straw and 51 Gold.*)

FOOTLIGHTS *or* F.O.H. SPOTS should be used to counteract shadows on the face. (FOOTLIGHTS *3 Straw and 51 Gold;* F.O.H. SPOTS *51 Gold.*)

SPOTS on No. 1 Bar immediately behind the proscenium should, if possible, be used for lighting the Acting Area. They should cover the table and chairs, L.C. (*3 Straw*); the settee, down L. (*3 Straw*); the door, up C. (*3 Straw*); the easy chair and the armchair (*3 Straw*). In addition one or more spots (*3 Straw and 17 Steel Blue together*) should be used to cover the area round the fireplace presumed to be lit by the gas brackets. (If two spots can be spared for this each should be linked to one gas bracket —in which a 15 watt lamp can be used—so that bracket and spot can be faded in and out together.)

FLOODS will be required to light the exterior backing. One FLOOD (*4 Amber*), placed off stage R., will be required to light the passage backing in ACT I. One small FLOOD (*2 Light Amber*), placed low down off stage R., will be required to light the cellar steps. A small SPOT, concealed in the fireplace will be required for the firelight. (*8 Salmon and 33 Deep Amber together.*)

If Borders are used instead of a Ceiling piece, it may be found necessary to use extra lighting behind them to avoid shadows on the tops of the set.

While SPOTS are not essential for the lighting of the play the atmosphere will be greatly assisted by their use. The light should be kept off the upper parts of the set and should be concentrated on the Acting Area in pools, leaving the corners of the stage in shadow. All circuits should be controlled by dimmers.

Where Cues are bracketed together they follow on almost continuously.

ACT I

Daylight. November afternoon. The curtains are open and the apparent source of light is from the window.

All SPOTS on; except SPOTS (*3 Straw and 17 Steel Blue*) covering fireplace.

BATTENS and FLOATS (*3 Straw and 51 Gold*) on check.

F.O.H. SPOTS on.

FLOOD (*4 Amber*) on passage backing from off R.

FLOODS (*3 Straw or 1 Yellow*) on exterior backing.

FIRE SPOT out.

Cue 1. Mrs Fearn. "You'd better." (*She exits.*)
Slow fade of Flood on passage backing. (*About 3 mins.*)
Slow fade in of Fire Spot.

Cue 2. George. "Take the bags upstairs! I won't be a tick!"
Slow fade of Battens and Floats; Floods on exterior
backing; Flood on passage backing; Spots covering
settee down l. and door up c. (*About 5 mins.*)

Cue 3. George *goes into the passage and strikes a match.*
Fade up Flood on passage backing for a moment, then
down again and slowly out. (*About 2 mins.*) Change
medium to *3 Straw* and *17 Steel Blue* together.

Cue 4. Alec *enters carrying lighted lantern.*
Fade up Spot (*3 Straw*) on door up c.

Cue 5. Alec *exits to cellar.*
Fade out Spot on door up c.

Cue 6. As Alec *steps through cellar door.*
Quick fade in of cellar Flood (*2 Light Amber*) on check.

Cue 7. As Alec "*descends cellar steps*".
Fade cellar Flood to out.

Cue 8. Francie. "Sssh! Be quiet! He's coming back!"
Slow fade in of cellar Flood.

Cue 9. As Alec *steps through cellar door.*
Quick fade out of cellar Flood.

Cue 10. As Alec *enters room.*
Fade in Spot on door up c. on check.

Cue 11. As Alec *exits.*
Fade out Spot on door up c.

Cue 12. George. "For heaven's sake, darling, be reasonable!"
Fade in Flood (*3 Straw and 17 Steel Blue*) on passage backing.

ACT II

Scene 1

Daylight. November morning. The curtains are open and the
apparent source of light is from the window.

All Spots on; except Spots (*3 Straw and 17 Steel Blue*) covering fireplace.

Battens and Floats (*3 Straw and 51 Gold*) full.

F.O.H. Spots on.

Flood (*4 Amber*) on passage backing from off r.

FLOODS (*56 Pale Chocolate*) on exterior backing.
FIRE SPOT on.

Cue 13.   *The* PROFESSOR *and* MADAM *go out.*
      Slow check of FLOODS on exterior backing; FLOOD on
      passage backing; BATTENS and FLOATS. (*About 4 mins.*)

Cue 14.   GEORGE. ". . . a pretty strong feeling that he didn't at all
      like what he saw . . ."
      Continue check, including SPOTS covering settee down L.
      door up C., and armchair and easy chair.

Cue 15.   *There is a loud rat-tat on the cellar door, and the next moment
      it is flung open.*
      Cellar FLOOD to be on ready for this entrance, on check.

Cue 16⎤ *As* ALEC *steps through cellar door.*
         Quick fade out of cellar FLOOD.

Cue 17⎱ *As* ALEC *enters the room.*
         Fade in SPOT on door up C.

Cue 18⎤ *As* ALEC *goes to cellar door.*
         Fade out SPOT on door up C.

Cue 19⎰ *As* ALEC *steps through cellar door.*
         Quick fade in of cellar FLOOD on check.

Cue 20⎱ *As* ALEC *"descends cellar steps".*
         Fade cellar FLOOD to out.

Cue 21.   GEORGE *lights the gas brackets on either side of the fireplace.*
      Fade in SPOTS (*3 Straw and 17 Steel Blue together*) to cover
      fireplace area. (*2 Stages.*)

SCENE 2

To open. As at end of SCENE 1. With the addition of the cellar
      FLOOD, just on, to light GEORGE dimly when he goes
      to the head of the cellar steps.

Cue 22.   GEORGE. ". . . Haunted house? Oh dear, Francie, what-
      ever next?" (*He starts to go to her.*)
      Quick fade of gas brackets, and covering SPOTS, to just on.

Cue 23⎤ GEORGE. ". . . He's coming up!"
         Fade in cellar FLOOD.

Cue 24⎱ *As* ALEC *steps through cellar door.*
         Quick fade out of cellar FLOOD.

Cue 25⎱ *As* ALEC *enters room.*
         Fade up SPOTS (*3 Straw*) to cover door up C. and easy
         chair.

Cue 26 ⎤ *As* ALEC *exits to passage.*
    ⎥ Fade SPOTS (*3 Straw*) covering door up c. and easy chair.
Cue 27 ⎰ *As* ALEC *steps through cellar door and "descends".*
    ⎱ Quick fade in of cellar FLOOD followed by slow fade out.
Cue 28. MRS BUTTERWORTH. ". . . Come in! Look sharp! I want
    you!"
    Quick fade up of gas brackets and covering SPOTS to
    opening light.

ACT III

To open. As at end of ACT II, SCENE 2. Except slight increase of
    light on garden backing.
Cue 29. *After* MADAM's *exit by window.*
    Change mediums for garden backing to 7 *Light Rose.*
Cue 30. PROFESSOR *opens curtains.*
    Fade up all SPOTS, BATTENS and FLOATS (*51 Gold*).

Note.—The colours indicated are intended only as a guide. The
actual colours employed must depend on the colour scheme of the
set and furnishings. They should be so chosen that differentiation
can be made between daylight and artificial light and it will
probably be found of advantage to colour the SPOTS for artificial
light and the BATTENS or FLOODS for daylight.